German Romantic Motets

Reger, Rheinberger, Schubert, Wagner and Wolf

Selected and edited by
Ralph Allwood

Phrase by phrase translations by
Elizabeth Robinson

Novello

Published in Great Britain by
Novello Publishing Limited

Head Office:
Novello & Company Limited
8/9 Frith Street, London W1D 3JB, England.
Telephone: +44 (0)20 7434 0066
Fax: +44 (0)20 7287 6329

Sales & Hire:
Music Sales Limited
Newmarket Road, Bury St Edmunds,
Suffolk IP33 3YB, England.
Telephone: +44 (0)1284 702600
Fax: +44 (0)1284 768301

Music setting by Chris Hinkins.

Front cover painting:
Gothic Cathedral by the Water, 1813,
Karl Friedrich Schinkel. Courtesy of AKG Images.
Back cover photograph:
Ralph Allwood by Tom Allwood. www.tomallwood.com

NOV078640
ISBN 1-84449-680-5

e-mail: music@musicsales.co.uk
www.chesternovello.com

Abendlied: German Romantic part-songs and anthems,
sung by the Rodolfus Choir conducted by Ralph Allwood,
is available on Herald AV Publications (HAVPCD 289).

Contents

Notes on the music

Max Reger

Abendlied

Reger's choral music, though substantial in quantity, has not always received the attention of his organ and orchestral music. The two pieces selected here come from opposite sides of his rather short, but highly productive, career. The *Abendlied* of 1899 dates from his years in Weiden with his family, where he had retreated after his wild youth in Wiesbaden, while by 1912, the date of *O Tod, wie bitter bist du,* he was settled in Leipzig as director of the Conservatory and enjoying his first real success as a composer. *Abendlied* belongs to a genre that had become popular in the nineteenth century, in which the drawing-on of evening became evocative of the sublime and the expression it called forth in the soul. Thus the poet here relates the returning home of tired people at the end of the day to the desire of the soul to make the 'ew'gen Flug ins Vaterhaus' ('final journey home'). Reger's intensely chromatic harmony is always there, though initially softened by the six smoothly flowing lines, and requires long-breathed phrasing to make its effect. The 'white veils of mist' and the accompanying silence are vividly depicted, while the soul's yearning provokes an impressive three-stage crescendo from bar 38 onwards.

O Tod, wie bitter bist du

As befits its text, *O Tod* is starker and less sumptuous – Reger makes powerful use of dissonance, as well as the sudden exposing of single lines. In this, as well as in the alternation of homophony and polyphony, and the dramatic use of silence after climaxes, the piece is arguably a Bruckner motet for the twentieth century – although the expressionist style is pushed almost into the operatic in passages such as bars 57-8. Reger sets the last section 'wie wohl tust du dem Dürftigen' ('how well you serve the needy person') to a serene chorale-like passage in E major, ignoring any possible irony in the text. A counterpart to this piece is the powerful *Trauerode* for organ of 1916 (the last year of his life), which charts a similar emotional trajectory.

Josef Rheinberger

Abendlied

Rheinberger is best known for his twenty organ sonatas. His choral music, however, has received little attention. Yet he composed prolifically, embracing many genres, and was a key figure in German musical life during the nineteenth century: Hans von Bülow recognised his prowess as a teacher and described him as 'one of the worthiest musicians and human beings in the world'. The recent publication of a fine complete edition should do much to rehabilitate his reputation, while the pieces gathered here give a representative picture of his style. He was essentially a conservative who, on the one hand, moved away from the rigidity of Cecilianism and, on the other, was cautious of the modernism of Liszt and Wagner. The charming *Abendlied*, the last of the *Drei geistliche Gesänge* Op. 69, was written, remarkably, when Rheinberger was only 15. Here the genre later used by Reger (see above) is appropriated for a sacred work: a setting of the disciples' words to the risen Jesus on the Emmaus road. Within its modest span the piece mixes rich chordal writing with Brahmsian imitative passages; the style overall is warmly diatonic.

Anima nostra (Unsere Seele)

In 1877 King Ludwig II of Bavaria, one-time patron of Wagner, appointed Rheinberger his court conductor for church music. For his new position he assembled a substantial collection of motets for use at different seasons of the liturgical year, some new, some already in existence. A selection is included here. *Anima nostra*, which has been called 'the high point of his motets', is set *a cappella* SSATTB – clearly a favourite texture of Rheinberger's. He makes no attempt at pictorial representation, but creates a rondo form (something surprisingly unusual in choral music) in which the opening figure recurs as a sort of lullaby for the Innocents commemorated in the liturgical feast.

Eripe me (Rette mich, Herr)

Eripe me is similar in mood to *Tribulationes* for its first half: a minor key with much use of the diminished seventh, and a dramatic unison gesture to begin. The form shows Rheinberger experimenting with structure: the opening theme is answered from bar 16 onwards by a second subject in the relative major portraying the psalmist's 'refuge' in a gentler, 'rocking' style. As the first idea reappears, there follows a sturdy fugato from bar 30 which affirms 'du bist mein Schöpfer und Gott!' ('you are my God'); and upon the third appearance of 'eripe', the second theme is then given in the tonic major before the quiet close.

Laudate dominum (Lobpreiset Gott den Herrn)

Employing once again a six-part texture, *Laudate Dominum* is an extrovert and impressive work. It is cast in ABA'B' form; the fanfare-like opening material effectively contrasting the upper and lower voices and this then answered from bar 9 onwards by flowing six-part counterpoint. Within this is contained a fugato on the words 'Quoniam suavis est', beginning with the first tenors and featuring a striking rising sixth. The contrapuntal texture here is handled with great skill, as the other parts decorate the fugal subject with their flowing lines.

Meditabor (Denken will ich)

This shorter Lenten motet falls into two parts, roughly corresponding with the sections of the offertory text. The first, appropriately for the penitential season, centres on a thoughtful, almost sombre D minor. Despite repeated pulls towards the warmer F major, it is only when Rheinberger modulates to D major that a true resolution 'ad mandata tua' ('dein Gesetz zu üben'; 'to greet your commands') is achieved.

Morgenlied

Another work from the Op. 69 set of 1858 is a balancing 'Morning Song', a more extended setting of a poem still essentially sacred though not biblical. It is reminiscent of Brahms's *Wo ist ein so herrlich Volk* (written in the same key of F major) in its cheerful optimism and sure handling of structure. Rheinberger modulates sharpwards at the mention of the nightingale, and introduces still more energetic writing for 'Sie singet Lob' ('she sings praise'). The most striking passage, however, occurs from bar 52 onwards, where the Lord's hand over the earth is depicted in downward chromatic lines in all voices. The opening material returns, closing with a sumptuous cadence from bar 100.

Tribulationes (Leiden und Bedrängnis)

Some of Rheinberger's motets include organ accompaniment, among them *Eripe me* and *Tribulationes*, eventually published in 1884. A certain tendency towards greater chromaticism is immediately apparent here – not so much dramatic modulations or intense dissonance, as the prevalence of circling figures using chromatic auxiliaries, creating an unsettled atmosphere. This is of course partly a response to the texts, which plead to God for rescue. *Tribulationes* opens with a winding downward curve from the organ, answered by a dramatic upward gesture from the choir; this dialectic continues until a new, somewhat more stable idea appears at bar 20 with the words 'vide humilitatem meam' ('see my humility'). The opening then returns in an altered form.

Franz Schubert

An die Musik

These two beautiful songs by Schubert here receive choral versions to stand alongside Cornelius' *Die Könige* (The Kings). Schubert was an early pioneer of the *a cappella* German Romantic choral tradition, as well as partsongs with piano, so such a treatment is not incongruous. *An die Musik* dates from 1817, when Schubert had already reached artistic maturity. His melody makes skilful use of the falling sixth throughout, as well as a gradual ascent, phrase by phrase, from E through F♯ to the high G♯ on 'Welt' ('world', v. 1). In this arrangement, the lower voice parts shadow and amplify the piano accompaniment.

Litanei auf das Fest Allerseelen

Schubert composed his *Litany for All Souls' Day* a year earlier, but it was published posthumously. A feature of Schubert's music is the three-bar epilogue, in which the keyboard part meditates, as it were, on the words just sung; this was a technique taken further by Schumann, whose piano epilogues sometimes carry much of the emotional weight of the song.

Zum Sanctus

As part of his large output of church music, Schubert wrote a number of settings in German rather than the conventional Latin. These include the *Deutsche Messe* written, along with an extraordinary amount of other music, in 1827 shortly before his death. Despite its brevity and simplicity, it immediately creates a devotional atmosphere, intensified by the extra repetitions of the word 'Heilig'. Schubert shows his unique skill at providing exquisite harmonic touches to colour a passage, such as the tenor D♭ in bar 10, which then steers the harmony in the other parts in bars 18 and 25.

Richard Wagner

An Webers Grabe

Among the young Richard Wagner's duties when he took up the position of assistant Kapellmeister in Dresden in 1843 was the composition of pieces for ceremonial occasions. One that he would have considered no chore was this piece to commemorate the return of Weber's remains to Dresden from England, where he had died from tuberculosis in 1826. Wagner, immensely indebted to Weber as a composer, had been a leading advocate of this event. He wrote the piece to his own text, in which can be heard echoes of the style of the later opera music dramas, and conducted it at the graveside. The music, falling in style somewhere between hymn- and lieder-like writing, forms part of a tradition of euphonious male-voice part songs which was notably contributed to by Schubert and Weber himself: indeed Weber's *Leyer und Schwert* were his first popular success. The music, mostly gently flowing, slows strikingly at the words 'denn hier ruh' Er' ('for here he rests').

Hugo Wolf

Aufblick

Wolf composed songs that are as unrivalled in their expression as they are unorthodox in their technique. Much of this stems from the influence of Wagner, whom he idolized all the more after meeting him and receiving encouragement. Most of the choral music dates from early in his career, including the *6 geistliche Lieder* written in April 1881. At their first publication after Wolf's death, the motets were heavily edited by Eugen Thomas. *Aufblick* (Looking upwards) opens the set with a bold flourish: Wolf portrays each change of emotion vividly without losing continuity, and closes with a splendid gesture of optimism. In bars 8-9, one can see the momentary idiosyncrasy of harmony in the bass that led Ernest Newman, while praising the set as 'intensely spiritual', to write that 'Wolf's technique and his faculty of expression are not yet quite the equals of his imagination'.

Ergebung

Though not the last of the set, *Ergebung* functions in some ways as an *Abschied* or 'leave-taking', with its stretched-out conclusion. It is no surprise to learn that it was sung at Wolf's funeral. The piece is noble and hymn-like in style, the regular phrase structure skilfully avoiding being repetitious by the turns of the harmony. Wolf sets 'O mit uns Sündern' ('O with us sinners') as a more urgent middle section, with the voices rising to a climax on 'Wehe' ('sorrow') before falling againat 'zum Staub' ('to the dust'). The opening then returns, developed marvellously with imitations towards the surprise G major chord of bar 43 – which sets up the long cadence in B major. Wolf added the last murmur of 'Dein Wille, Herr, geschehe!' ('May your will, Lord, be done!') some years later in 1899.

Letzte Bitte

Letzte Bitte ('Last Prayer') has always been admired. The downward chromatic bass line with which *Aufblick* opens here becomes a pervasive presence in the first twelve bars, depicting the weariness of the 'mortally-wounded' speaker, as each phrase sinks downwards as though in quicksand. Only in bar 13, its mention of God, is a more positive mood established, climaxing in the sopranos' high G♯ at the words 'endlich Frieden' ('peace finally'), before a sombre resolution is achieved with the closing bare fifth.

David Goode

dem 'Philharmonischen Chor' (Berlin) und seinem verdienstvollen Dirigenten
Herrn Professor Siegfried Ochs hochachtungsvollst zugeeignet

Abendlied

August H. Plinke

Max Reger (1873–1916)
Drei sechsstimmige Chöre, Op. 39, no. 2

crimson for the last time glows the forest,

as if kissed by the burning sun with its golden

13
poco a poco stringendo
Strahl. Weis - se Ne-bel-schlei-er stei - gen,
Strahl. Weis - se Ne - bel - schlei - er stei - gen
Strahl. Weis - se Ne - bel-schlei - er
Strahl. Weis - se Ne - bel-schlei-er stei-gen wal - lend, wal -
Strahl. Weis - se Ne - bel-schlei-er stei - gen wal - lend, wal-
Strahl. Weis - se Ne - bel - schlei-er stei - gen wal - -
poco a poco stringendo
ray. White veils of mist rise upwards

rit.
a tempo
17
mf
f
pp
ppp
p
stei-gen wal - lend aus dem See em-por.
wal - - - lend aus dem See em-por. Rings ist Stil - le,
stei - gen wal - lend aus dem See em-por. Rings ist
-lend, wal - lend aus dem See em - por. Rings ist Stil - le,
- lend aus dem See em - por. Rings ist
-lend, stei-gen wal - lend aus dem See em - por. Rings ist
rit.
a tempo
swirling from the ocean.
All around is only

stillness and silence, *Calm and no*

25
meno pp
Laut klingt an mein Ohr. Und es stre - ben
meno pp
Laut klingt an mein Ohr. Und es stre - ben al -
Laut klingt an mein Ohr, kein Laut klingt an mien Ohr.
und kein Laut klingt an mein Ohr, und kein Laut klingt an mein
meno pp
Laut klingt an mein Ohr. Und es stre - ben,
meno pp
Laut klingt an mein Ohr. Und es stre - ben
sound is heard in my ear.
And all

tired souls are now striving to return home.

32
mp
Denn der A - ben lockt mit
Hei - mat zu. Denn der A - bend lockt mit
Hei - mat zu. Denn der A - bend lockt mit
Hei - mat zu. Denn der A - bend
Hei - mat zu. Denn der A - - bend lockt mit
Hei - mat zu. Denn der A - bend lockt mit
For the evening beckons with

35
più p
ppp
Frie - den und die Nacht mit süs - - ser Ruh.
più p
pp
Frie - den und die Nacht mit süs - - ser Ruh.
più p
pp
Frie - den und die Nacht mit süs - - ser Ruh.
più pp
pp
lockt mit Frie - den und die Nacht mit süs - ser Ruh.
più p
pp
Frie - den, die Nacht mit süs - - ser Ruh.
più p
pp
Frie - den, die Nacht mit süs - - ser Ruh.
peace and the night with sweet rest.

And in far off realms

my soul surges out,

just as if it wanted to prepare itself

for the final journey

rit.
51
fff p più p ppp
Va - - ter - haus, zum Flug ins Va - - ter-haus.
fff p più p ppp
Va - - ter - haus, zum Flug ins Va - - ter-haus.
fff p più p ppp
Va - - ter - haus, zum Flug ins Va - ter - haus.
hervortreten
fff p più p ppp
Va - ter - haus, zum ew' - gen Flug ins Va - ter - haus.
fff p più p ppp
Va - ter - haus, zum ew' - gen Flug ins Va - ter - haus.
fff p più p ppp
Va - - ter - haus, zum Flug ins Va - ter - haus.
rit.
home.

Dem Andenken von Frau Lili Wach, geb. Mendelssohn-Bartholdy

O Tod, wie bitter bist du

Ecclesiasticus, ch. 41, vv. 1–2

Max Reger (1873–1916)
Geistliche Gesänge, Op. 110, no. 3

when a man thinks of you,

who has good days and sufficient,

(stringendo)
rit.
16
Ta - ge und ge - nug hat, ge -
- nug hat, ge -
meno ff
wenn an dich ge - den - ket ein Mensch und oh - ne Sor - gen
gu - te, gu - te Ta - ge hat,
Mensch, der gu - te Ta - ge hat,
rit.
and lives without worries;
(rit.)
a tempo
poco
poco rit.
19
-nug hat, und oh - ne Sor - gen le - bet;
- nug hat, und oh - ne, oh - ne Sor - gen
le - bet, und oh - ne Sor - gen
poco espress.
ge - nug hat, und oh - ne Sor - gen
und oh - ne Sor - gen, und oh - ne Sor - gen
a tempo
poco rit.

(poco rit.)
a tempo
stringendo
o - Tod, wie bit - ter bist du, wie bit - ter, wie bit - ter, wie
le - bet;
wie_ bit - ter, wie bit - ter, wie
wie bit - ter, wie_ bit - ter, wie
wie bit - ter, wie bit - ter, wie
rit.
a tempo
rit.
bit - ter, wie_ bit - ter, wie_ bit - ter bist du,
(non dim.)
wie bit - ter bist

and who is at ease in all things

rit.
a tempo
39
und wohl noch es - sen mag! O Tod, wie
und wohl noch es - sen mag! O Tod, wie
und wohl noch es - sen mag! O Tod,
und wohl noch es - sen mag! O
und wohl noch es - sen mag!
rit.
a tempo
and may still eat well!
42
bit - ter, o Tod, wie bit - ter, wie
bit - ter, wie
o Tod, wie bit - ter,
Tod, o Tod, wie bit - ter,
O Tod, wie bit - ter,

46
stringendo
bit - ter, o Tod, wie
bit - ter, wie bit - ter, o Tod, wie
o Tod, wie bit - ter, o Tod, wie
o Tod, o Tod, o Tod, wie
o Tod, o Tod, wie
stringendo
51
rit.
a tempo
bit - ter, wie bit - ter, o Tod, wenn an dich ge-den-ket ein
bit - ter, wie bit - ter, o Tod, o Tod,
bit - ter, wie bit - ter, o Tod, wenn an dich ge-den-ket ein
bit - ter, wie bit - ter, o Tod, wenn an dich ge-den-ket ein
bit - ter, wie bit - ter, o Tod, wenn an dich ge-den-ket ein
rit.
a tempo

56
pp
f
mf
Mensch,
wie bit - ter,
o Tod,
espress.
Mensch,
o — Tod,
o — Tod,
o Tod,
wie bit - ter, wie bit - ter,
wie

60
stringendo
ppp
mp
o Tod, wie bit - ter, wie —
wie bit - ter,
o —
bit - ter,
o Tod,
o Tod,
stringendo

(stringendo)
rit.
a tempo
64
ff
bit - ter, wie bit - ter, wie bit - ter, bit - ter, bit - -
Tod, o Tod, wie bit - - - - - ter, wie
Tod, o Tod, o Tod, wie bit - ter, bit - ter,
o Tod, o Tod, wie bit - ter bist
o Tod, wie bit - ter, wie
68
pp
- ter bist du, wie bit - ter bist
bit - ter bist du, wie bit - ter bist
bit - ter bist du, wie bit - ter bist
espress.
p
mp
du, wie bit - ter bist du, wie bit - ter, wie bit - ter bist
bit - ter bist du, wie bit - ter bist

Molto largo (♪ = 60)
73
ppp espress.
poco
ppp
p
du, o Tod! O Tod, wie wohl tust du, wie wohl tust
du, o Tod! O Tod, wie wohl tust du, wie wohl tust
du, o Tod! O Tod, wie wohl tust du,_ wie_ wohl tust_
du, o Tod! O Tod, wie_ wohl tust du, wie wohl tust_
du, o Tod! O Tod, wie wohl tust du, wie wohl tust_
Molto largo (♪ = 60)
O death, how well you serve
77
mf
pp
ppp
du dem Dürf - ti - gen, der da schwach und alt ist,
du dem_ Dürf - ti - gen, der_ da schwach und alt ist,
du dem Dürf - ti - gen, der da schwach und alt ist,
du dem Dürf - ti - gen, der da_ schwach und alt_ ist,
du_ dem_ Dürf - ti - gen, der da schwach und_ alt ist,
the needy person,
who is weak and old,

who has every care, and cannot

hope or expect anything better.

86
ppp
mp
Tod, wie wohl tust du, wie wohl tust du, o
Tod, wie wohl tust du, wie wohl tust du, wie wohl tust
Tod, wie wohl tust du, wie wohl tust du, o
Tod wie wohl tust du, wie wohl tust du, o
Tod wie wohl tust du, wie wohl tust du, wie
89
rit.
a tempo
rit.
mf
pp dolciss.
Tod, o Tod, wie wohl tust du, wie wohl tust du.
du, o Tod, wie wohl, wie wohl tust du.
Tod, o Tod, wie wohl, wie wohl tust du.
Tod, o Tod, wie wohl, wie wohl tust du.
wohl, wie wohl, wie wohl, wie wohl tust du.

Abendlied

Luke ch. 24, v. 29

Josef Rheinberger (1839–1901)
Drei geistliche Gesänge, Op. 69, no. 3

Remain with us, for it is becoming evening,

6
bleib bei uns, denn es will A - bend wer -
bei uns, denn es will A - bend wer -
f
bleib bei uns, denn es will A - bend wer -
f
denn es will
f
bleib bei uns, denn es will,
f
bleib bei uns, denn es will A - bend, A - bend wer -
11
f
ff
- den, denn es will A - bend wer - den, A -
f
- den, denn es will A - bend wer -
f
- den, denn es will
A - bend wer - - den, denn es will A -
f
denn es will A - bend wer - den, will A -
f
- den, denn es will A -

16
dim.
f
- bend wer - den, und der Tag hat sich ge - nei -
- den, A - bend wer - den, und der Tag hat sich ge -
A - bend wer - den,
- bend wer - den,
- bend wer - den, und der
- bend wer - den,
and the day has ended.
22
- get, sich ge - nei - - - - - get, sich ge -
- nei - - - - get, sich ge - nei - - -
und der Tag hat sich ge - nei - - get, hat sich ge -
und der Tag hat sich ge - nei -
Tag hat sich ge - nei - - - - get, hat sich ge -
und der Tag hat sich ge - nei - get, sich ge -

27
-nei - get, bleib bei uns, denn es will A - bend
- - get, bleib bei uns, denn es will A - bend
-nei - get, o bleib bei uns, denn es will A - bend
- - - get, bleib bei uns, denn es will A-bend
-nei - - get, o bleib bei uns, denn es will A-bend
-nei - - get, bleib bei uns, denn es will A-bend
32
wer - den, und der Tag hat sich ge -
wer - den, und der Tag hat
wer - den, und der Tag hat sich ge - nei -
wer - den, und der Tag hat sich ge -
wer - den, und der Tag hat sich ge - neigt, hat sich ge -
wer - den, und der Tag hat sich ge - nei - get, hat sich ge -

38
p
f
-nei - get. O bleib bei uns, o bleib bei uns, o
mf
f
sich ge-nei - get. O bleib bei uns, bleib, o
-get. O bleib bei uns, bei uns, o bleib, o
-nei - get. O bleib bei uns, bei uns, denn es will A - bend
-nei - get. O bleib bei uns, o bleib, o
-nei - get. O bleib, o bleib bei uns, o bleib, o
44
ff
dim.
pp
bleib bei uns, denn es will A - bend wer - den.
bleib bei uns, denn es will A - bend wer - den.
bleib bei uns, denn es will A - bend wer - den.
wer - den, denn es will A - bend wer - den.
bleib bei uns, denn es will A - bend wer - den.
bleib bei uns, denn es will A - bend wer - den.

Anima nostra
(Unsere Seele)

Offertory for the Feast of the Innocents

Josef Rheinberger (1839–1901)
4 Sechsstimmige Motetten, Op. 133, no. 1

Our soul, like a sparrow, has been set free

from the hunter's snare.

12
p
ve-nan - ti - um. A-ni-ma no-stra, si - cut pas-ser.
der sie ver - folgt. Un-se - re See- le, gleich dem Sper-ling.
p f
- um. A - ni-ma no-stra, si - cut pas-ser e - rep-ta
- folgt. Un - se - re See - le, gleich dem Sper-ling ward sie be -
p f
- um. A - ni-ma no - stra, si - cut pas - ser e - rep-ta
- folgt. Un - se - re See - le, gleich dem Sper - ling ward sie be -
p f
- um. A - ni-ma no - stra, si - cut pas-ser e - rep-ta
- folgt. Un - se - re See - le, gleich dem Sper-ling ward sie be -
p f
- um. A - ni-ma no - stra, si - cut pas-ser e -
- folgt. Un - se - re See - le, gleich dem Sper-ling ward
p f
- um. A - ni-ma no - stra, si - cut pas - ser e - rep-ta
- folgt. Un - se - re See - le, gleich dem Sper - ling ward sie be -

The snare is broken and

we have been set free.

27
f
p
nos li - be - ra - ti su - mus. A - ni - ma no - stra, si - cut
vom Feind sind wir er - ret - tet. Un - se - re See - le, gleich dem
nos li - be - ra - ti su - mus. A - ni - ma no - stra,
Fein - de sind wir er - ret - tet. Un - se - re See - le,
nos li - be - ra - ti su - mus. A - ni - ma no - stra, e - rep - ta
Fein - de sind wir er - ret - tet. Un - se - re See - le, ward be - freit,
p dolce
nos li - be - ra - ti su - mus. A - ni - ma no - stra, no - stra, e -
Fein - de sind wir er - ret - tet. Un - se - re See - le, sie ward, sie
nos li - be - ra - ti su - mus. A - ni - ma no - stra, si - cut pas - ser,
vom Feind sind wir er - ret - tet. Un - se - re See - le, gleich dem Sper - ling,
nos li - be - ra - ti su - mus. A - ni - ma no - stra, e - rep - ta
Fein - de sind wir er - ret - tet. Un - se - re See - le, ward be - freit,

Our help in overcoming all fears is

from the name of the Lord who made heaven and earth.

45
-to - ri-um no - strum. qui
Ban - gen der Er - de. wird
in no - mi-ne Do - mi - ni, qui fe - cit
wird Hil - fe von Gott al - lein, wird Hil - fe
-to - ri - um no - strum in no - mi - ne Do - mi - ni, qui fe - cit, qui
Ban -gen der Er - de wird Hil - fe von Gott al - lein, wird Hil - fe von
-to - ri - um no - strum in no - mi - ne Do - mi - ni, qui fe - cit, qui
Ban -gen der Er - de wird Hil - fe von Gott al - lein, wird Hil - fe von
Ad - ju - to - ri - um no-strum in no - mi - ne, qui fe - cit
Je - dem Ban - gen der Er - de wird Hil - fe, wird Hil - fe,
-to - ri - um no - strum in no - mi - ne Do - mi - ni, qui fe - cit, qui
Ban -gen der Er - de wird Hil - fe von Gott al - lein, wird Hil - fe, wird

50
f
p
fe - cit coe - lum et ter - ram.
A - ni-ma
Hil - fe, Hil - fe von Gott al - lein.
Un-se - re
f
p dolce
coe - lum et ter - ram.
A - ni-ma no - stra,
von Gott, von Gott al - lein.
Un - se - re See - le,
f
p
fe - cit coe - lum et ter - ram.
A - ni-ma no - stra,
Gott al - lein, von Gott al - lein.
Un - se - re See - le,
f
p
fe - cit coe - lum et ter - ram.
A - ni-ma no - stra,
Gott al - lein, von Gott al - lein.
Un - se - re See - le,
f
mf
coe-lum et ter - ram, et ter - ram.
e -
Hil - fe von Gott, von Gott al - lein.
ward
f
p
fe - cit coe - lum et ter - ram.
A - ni-ma no - stra,
Hil - fe von Gott, von Gott al - lein.
Un - se - re See - le,

57
f
no - stra, si - cut pas - ser e - rep - ta, e - rep - ta
See - le, gleich dem Sper - ling ward sie, ward sie be -
si - cut pas - ser e - rep - ta est.
gleich dem Sper - ling ward sie be - freit.
Al - le -
si - cut pas - ser e - rep - ta est, si - cut pas -
gleich dem Sper - ling ward sie be - freit, gleich dem Sper -
si - cut pas - ser e - rep - ta est, e - rep - ta
gleich dem Sper - ling ward sie be - freit, ward sie be -
- rep - ta est.
sie be - freit.
Al - le - lu -
si - cut pas - ser e - rep - ta, e - rep - ta est, e -
gleich dem Sper - ling ward sie, ward sie be - freit, ward

Alleluia.

62
ff
est. Al-le - lu - ja, al - le - lu - ja, al -
-freit,
- lu - ja, al - le - lu - ja, al - le - lu - ja,
-ser e - rep - ta est. Al - le - lu - ja, al - le -
-ling ward sie be - freit.
est. Al - le - lu - ja, al - le - lu - ja,
-freit.
- ja, al - le - lu - ja, al - le - lu - ja,
- rep - ta est. Al - le - lu - ja, al - le -
sie be - freit.

67
p
- le - lu - - - - ja. A - ni-ma
Un - se - re
p dolce
al - le - lu - ja. A - ni-ma no - stra,
Un - se - re See - le,
p
- lu - ja, al - le - lu - - ja. A - ni-ma no - stra,
Un - se - re See - le,
p
al - le - lu - jah, al - le - lu - - ja. A - ni - ma
Un - se - re
p
al - le - lu - - - ja. A - ni-ma no - stra,
Un - se - re See - le,
p
- lu - - ja, al - le - lu - ja. A - ni-ma no - stra,
Un - se - re See - le,

72
no - stra, si - cut pas - ser e - rep - ta est, e - rep - ta
See - le, gleich dem Sper - ling ward sie be - freit, ward sie be -
si - cut pas - ser e - rep - ta, e - rep - ta est, e - rep - ta
gleich dem Sper - ling ward sie be - frei - et, ward sie, ward sie be -
si - cut pas - ser e - rep - ta est, e - rep - ta
gleich dem Sper - ling ward sie be - freit, ward sie be -
no - stra, si - cut pas - ser e - rep - ta est, e - rep - ta
See - le, gleich dem Sper - ling ward sie be - freit, ward sie be -
si - cut pas - ser e - rep - ta est, e - rep - ta
gleich dem Sper - ling ward sie be - freit, ward sie be -
si - cut pas - ser e - rep - ta est, e - rep - ta est.
gleich dem Sper - ling ward sie be - freit, ward sie be - freit.

78
p
est. A-ni-ma no-stra, si - cut pas-ser
-freit. Un-se-re See - le, gleich dem Sper-ling
p f
est. A-ni-ma no-stra, si - cut pas-ser e - rep - ta
-freit. Un-se-re See - le, gleich dem Sper-ling ward sie be -
p f
est. A-ni-ma no-stra, si - cut pas-ser e - rep - ta
-freit. Un-se-re See - le, gleich dem Sper-ling ward sie be -
p
est. A - ni-ma no-stra, si - cut pas-ser
-freit. Un - se-re See - le, gleich dem Sper-ling
sf p f
est. A - ni-ma no-stra, si - cut pas-ser e - rep - ta
-freit. Un - se-re See - le, gleich dem Sper-ling ward sie be -
p f
A - ni - ma no - stra, si - cut pas- ser, si - cut pas - ser e -
Un - se - re See - le, gleich dem Sper - ling, gleich dem Sper - ling ward

84
Adagio
f
pp
e - rep - ta est, e - rep - ta est.
ward sie be - freit, ward sie___ be - freit.
est, e - rep - ta est, e - rep - ta est.
-freit, ward sie___ be - freit, ward sie be - freit.
est,___ e - rep - ta est, e - rep - ta est.
-freit,___ ward sie be - freit, ward sie be - freit.
e - rep - ta est, e - rep - ta est.
ward sie be - freit, ward___ sie be - freit.
est, e - rep - ta est, e - rep - ta est.
-freit, ward sie___ be - freit, ward sie be - freit.
-rep - ta, e - rep - ta est, e - rep - ta est.
sie, ward sie be - freit, ward sie be - freit.
Adagio

Eripe me
(Rette mich, Herr)

Psalm 142, v. 11

Josef Rheinberger (1839–1901)
5 Hymnen, Op. 140, no. 3

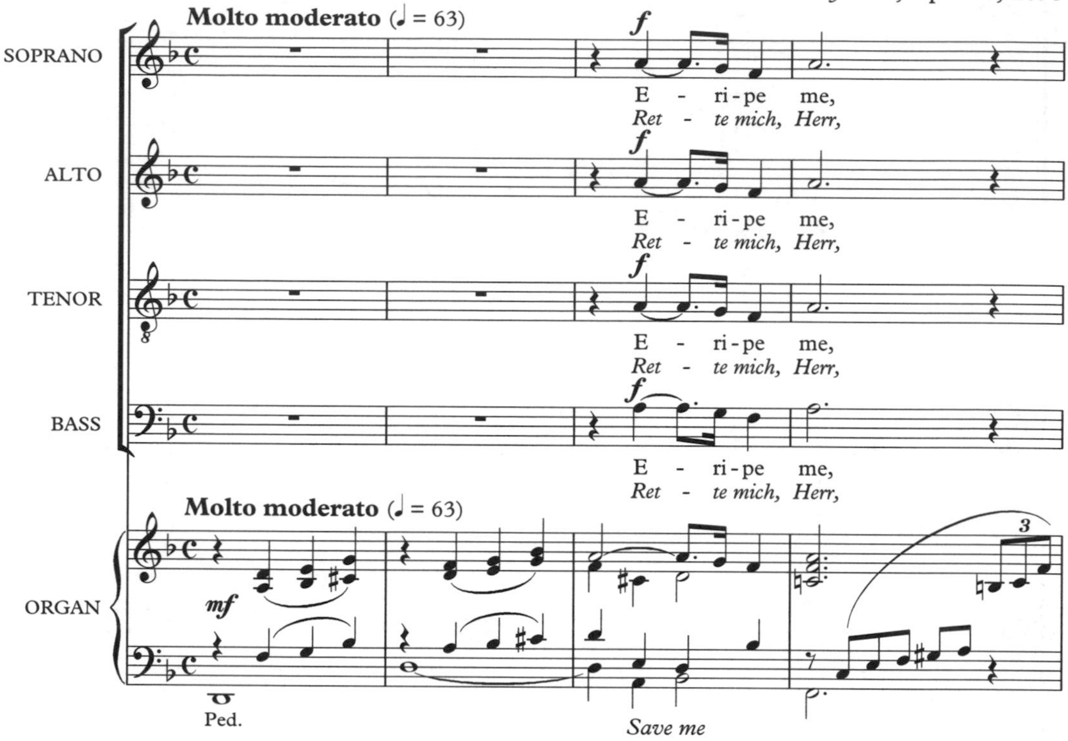

9
mf
me de i - ni-mi-cis me-is, de i - ni-mi-cis
Herr, vom Fein - de mei-ner See-le, vom Fein - de mei-ner
p
de i - ni - mi - cis_ me - is, de i - ni - mi - cis_
vom Fein - de mei - ner_ See - le, vom Fein - de mei - ner_
de i - ni - mi - cis me - is, de i - ni - mi - cis
vom Fein - de mei - ner See - le, vom Fein - de mei - ner
Ped.
from my enemies,
13
f
ff
p dolce
me - is, Do - mi - ne, Do - mi - ne! Ad
See - le, ret - te mich, Gott_ und Herr! Zu
me - is, Do - mi - ne, Do - mi - ne, Do-mi - ne! Ad
See - le, ret - te mich, Gott und Herr! Zu
me - is, Do - mi - ne, Do - mi - ne! Ad
See - le, ret - te mich, Gott_ und Herr! Zu
mf
Man.
Lord!

17
p
te con - fu - gi, do - ce - me fa - ce -
dir ent - flieh' ich, hel - fe mir, leh - re
te con - fu - gi, do - ce me fa - ce -
dir ent - flieh' ich, hel - fe mir, leh - re
dolce
te con - fu - gi, do - ce me, do - ce me fa - ce -
dir ent - flieh' ich, hel - fe mir, hel - fe mir, leh - re
te con - fu - gi, do - ce me fa - ce -
dir ent - flieh' ich, hel - fe mir, leh - re
mf
I fly to you for refuge, help me, teach me

22
f
-re vo - lun-ta-tem tu-am, fa-ce - re vo - lun-ta-tem tu - am.
mich dein Ge-setz zu hal-ten, leh-re mich dein Ge-setz zu hal - ten.
-re vo-lun-ta - tem tu-am, fa-ce - re vo-lun-ta - tem tu - am.
mich dein Ge-setz zu hal-ten, leh-re mich dein Ge-setz zu hal - ten.
-re vo-lun-ta - tem tu - am, fa-ce - re vo-lun-ta - tem tu - am.
mich dein Ge-setz zu hal - ten, leh-re mich dein Ge-setz zu hal - ten.
-re vo-lun-ta - tem tu-am, vo-lun - ta - tem tu - am.
mich dein Ge-setz zu hal-ten, dein Ge - setz zu hal - ten.
p
to do your will.
Ped.

26
p
f
mf
E - ri-pe me, e - ri-pe
Ret - te mich, Herr, ret - te mich,
E - ri-pe me, e - ri-pe me,
Ret - te mich, Herr, ret - te mich, Herr.
Save me,
30
me, qui - a De - us me - us es tu,
Herr! Denn du bist mein Schöp-fer und Gott,
me, qui - a De - us me - us es tu,
Herr! Denn du bist mein Schöp-fer und Gott,
me, qui - a De - us, qui - a De - us me - us es tu,
Herr! Denn du bist mein Schöp-fer, bist mein Schöp-fer und Gott,
qui - a De - us me - us es tu, qui - a De - us
Denn du bist mein Schöp-fer und Gott, denn du bist mein
Man.
for you are my God.

34
qui - a De - us me - us es tu,
denn du bist mein Schöp - fer und Gott,
qui - a De - us me - us es tu, qui - - a
denn du bist mein Schöp-fer und Gott, denn du
qui - a De - us me - us, qui - a De - us es tu,
denn du bist mein Schöp - fer, bist mein Schöp - fer und Gott,
me - us es tu, qui - a De - us me - us es
Schöp - fer und Gott, denn du bist mein Schöp - fer und
37
qui - a De - us me - us es tu.
denn du bist mein Schöp - fer und Gott!
De - us me - us, qui - a De - us es tu.
bist mein Schöp - fer, bist mein Gott, bist mein Gott!
f
qui - a De - us, qui - a De - us me - us es tu.
denn du bist mein Schöp - fer, bist mein Schöp - fer und Gott!
tu, qui - a De - us me - us es tu. E - ri - pe
Gott, denn du bist mein Schöp - fer und Gott! Ret - te mich,

40
E - ri - pe me, qui - a De - us me - us es
Ret - te mich, Herr, denn du bist mein Schöp - fer und
E - ri - pe me, e - ri - pe me, qui - a De - us me - us es
Ret - te mich, Herr, ret - te mich, Herr, denn du bist mein Schöp - fer und
E - ri - pe, e - ri - pe, qui - a De - us qui - a De - us me - us es
Ret - te mich, ret - te mich, ret - te mich, du bist mein Schöp - fer, du bist mein
me, e - ri - pe, qui - a De - us me - us, De - us me - us es
Herr, ret - te mich, denn du bist mein Herr Gott, bist mein Schöp - fer ind
(Man.)
Ped.
44
p doce
tu. Do - ce me
Gott. Hel - fe mir,
tu. Ad te con - fu - gi, do - ce me fa - ce-
Gott. Zu dir ent - flieh' ich, hel - fe mir, leh - re
tu. Ad te con - fu - gi, do - ce me
Gott. Zu dir ent - flieh' ich, hel - fe mir,
tu. Ad te con - fu - gi, do - ce me
Gott. Zu dir ent - flieh' ich, hel - fe mir,
Man.

48
mf f sf
fa - ce - re vo - lun-ta-tem tu-am, qui - a De - us
leh - re mich dein Ge-setz zu hal-ten, denn du bist mein
f
-re vo-lun-ta - tem, vo-lun-ta - tem tu-am, qui - a De - us
mich, leh-re mich, Herr, dein Ge-setz zu hal-ten, denn du bist mein
f
fa - ce - re vo-lun-ta - tem tu - am, qui - a
leh - re mich dein Ge-setz zu hal - ten, denn du
f
fa - ce - re vo-lun-ta - tem tu - am, qui - a De - us
leh - re mich dein Ge-setz zu hal - ten, denn du bist mein
Ped.
52
sf f ff p
me - us es tu, e - ri-pe me, e - ri-pe me, qui - a
Schöp - fer und Gott! ret - te mich, Herr! ret - te mich, Herr, denn mein
sf f ff p
me - us es tu, e - ri-pe me, e - ri-pe me, qui - a
Schöp - fer und Gott! ret - te mich, Herr! ret - te mich, Herr, denn mein
sf f ff p
De - us me - us es tu, e - ri-pe me, e - ri-pe me, qui - a
bist mein Schöp-fer und Gott! ret - te mich, Herr! ret - te mich, Herr, denn mein
sf f ff p
me - us es tu, e - ri-pe me, e - ri-pe me, qui - a
Schöp - fer und Gott! ret - te mich, Herr! ret - te mich, Herr, denn mein
f p

56
cresc.
f
De - us me - us es tu, qui - a De - us me - us es
Gott, mein Schöp - fer bist du, denn mein Gott, mein Schöp - fer bist
De - us me - us es tu, e - ri-pe me, e - ri-pe
Gott, mein Schöp - fer bist du, ret - te mich, Herr, ret - te mich,
De - us me - us es tu, e - ri-pe me,
Gott, mein Schöp - fer bist du, ret - te mich, Herr,
De - us me - us es tu, es tu, e -
Gott, mein Schöp - fer bist du, bist du, ret -
60
rit.
p
tu, qui - a De - us me - us es tu.
du, denn mein Gott, mein Schöp - fer bist du.
me, qui - a De - us me - us es tu.
Herr, denn mein Gott, mein Schöp - fer bist du.
qui - a De - us me - us es tu.
denn mein Gott, mein Schöp - fer bist du.
- ri-pe me, qui - a De - us me - us es tu.
- te mich, Herr, denn mein Gott, mein Schöp - fer bist du.

Laudate Dominum
(Lobpreiset Gott den Herrn)

Psalm 134, vv. 3, 6

Josef Rheinberger (1839–1901)
4 Sechsstimmige Motetten, Op. 133, no. 3

4
- ig - nus est, psal - li - te no - mi-ni e - jus, psal - li - te
-her - zig ist, und gross und herr - lich sein Na - me, lob - prei - set
- ig - nus est, psal - li - te no - mi-ni e - jus, psal - li - te
-her - zig ist, und gross und herr - lich sein Na - me, lob - prei - set
- ig - nus est, psal - li - te no - mi-ni e - jus, psal - li - te
-her - zig ist, und gross und herr - lich sein Na - me, lob - prei - set
qui - a ben - ig - nus est, psal - li - te no - mi - ni
weil er barm - her - zig ist, und gross und herr - lich sein
qui - a ben - ig - nus est, psal - li - te, psal - li - te no - mi - ni
weil er barm - her - zig ist, lob - prei - set, weil gross und herr - lich sein
qui - a ben - ig - nus est, psal - li - te no - mi - ni
weil er barm - her - zig ist, und gross und herr - lich sein
kind, sing to his name.

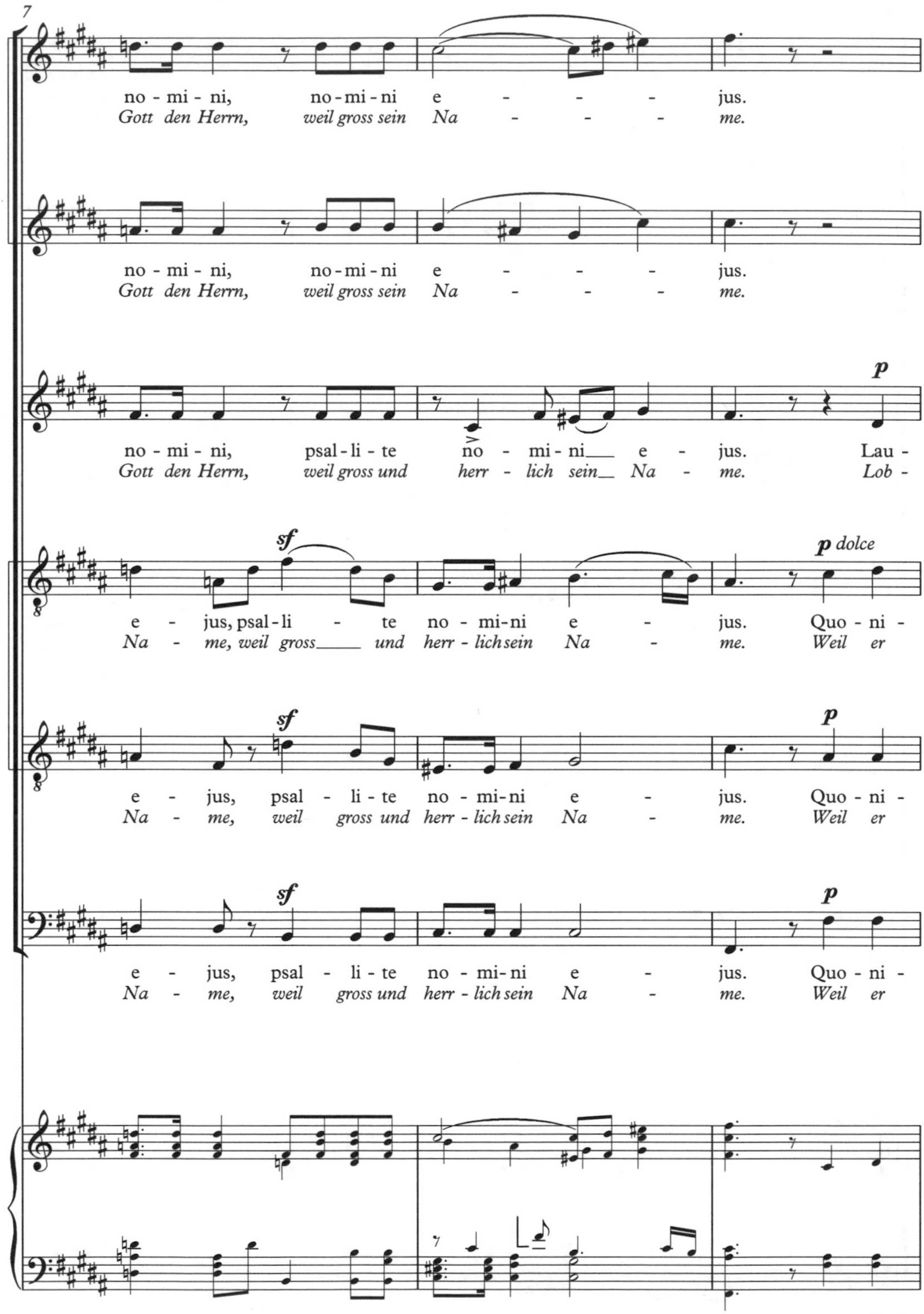
7
no - mi - ni, no - mi - ni e - - - jus.
Gott den Herrn, weil gross sein Na - - - me.
no - mi - ni, no - mi - ni e - - - jus.
Gott den Herrn, weil gross sein Na - - - me.
p
no - mi - ni, psal - li - te no - mi - ni e - jus. Lau -
Gott den Herrn, weil gross und herr - lich sein Na - me. Lob -
sf p dolce
e - jus, psal - li - te no - mi - ni e - jus. Quo - ni -
Na - me, weil gross und herr - lich sein Na - me. Weil er
sf p
e - jus, psal - li - te no - mi - ni e - jus. Quo - ni -
Na - me, weil gross und herr - lich sein Na - me. Weil er
sf p
e - jus, psal - li - te no - mi - ni e - jus. Quo - ni -
Na - me, weil gross und herr - lich sein Na - me. Weil er

Praise

the Lord for he is lovable.

13
f
- da - te, quo - ni - am su - a - - - -
- prei - set, weil er all - barm - her - - - -
- da - te Do - mi - num, lau - da - te,
- prei - set den Herrn, lob - prei - set,
f
est, quo - ni - am su - a - vis est, quo - ni -
ist, weil er all - barm-her - zig ist, weil er
f
est, lau - da - te Do - - - - mi -
ist, lob - prei - set Gott, Gott den
- da - te Do - mi - num qui - a ben - ig - nus est, qui - a ben - ig -
- prei - set Gott den Herrn, weil er barm-her-zig ist, weil er barm-her -
f
Lau - da - te, lau - da - te Do - mi -
Lob - prei - set, lob - prei - set Gott den

16
- vis__ est, psal - li - te____ no-mi-ni
- zig__ ist, gross____ und herr - lich ist sein
lau - - da - te,____ lau - da - te,
lob - - prei - set____ lob - prei - set,
- am, su - a - vis est, lau - da - te, lau - da -
all - barm her - zig ist, lob - prei - set, lob- prei -
- num, quo - ni - am su - a - vis
Herrn, weil er all - barm-her - zig
- nus__ est, ben - ig - nus__ est, psal -
- zig__ ist, barm - her - zig__ ist, herr -
- num, qui - a ben - ig - nus__ est, qui - a ben -
Herrn, weil er barm - her - zig__ ist, weil____ er barm -

19
f
e - jus, psal - li - te no- mi - ni
Na - me, gross und herr - lich ist sein
f
quo - ni - am su - a - vis est,
weil er all - barm-her - zig ist,
- te, lau- da - - - - - - te, lau- da -
- set, lob- prei - - - - - - set, lob- prei -
f
est, lau - da - te Do - - mi -
ist, lob - prei - set ihn, lob - prei - set
- li - te no - - ni - ni e - jus, lau -
- lich und gross ist sein Na - me, lob -
f
- ig - nus est, ben - ig - nus est, lau - da - te
- her - zig ist, barm - her - zig ist, lob - prei - set

22
e - jus, psal - li - te no - mi - ni e - jus,
Na - me, gross und herr - lich sein Na - me,
psal - li - te no - mi - ni e - jus, quo - ni -
herr - lich und gross ist sein Na - me, weil er
- te Do - mi - num, lau - da - - - -
- set Gott den Herrn, lob - prei - - -
-num, lau - da - te,
ihn, lob - prei - set,
-da - te, lau - da - te Do - mi - num, quo - ni -
-prei - set, lob - prei - set sei - nen Na - men, weil
Do - - mi - num, quo - ni - am su - a - vis
Gott den Herrn, weil er all - barm - her - zig
f
ff

25
ff
quo - ni - am su - a - vis est.
weil er all - barm-her - zig ist.
- am su - a - vis est.
all - - barm - her - - zig ist.
- te quo - ni - am su - a - vis est.
- set, weil er all - barm - her - zig ist.
p
su - a - vis est. O - mni-
barm- her - zig ist. Al - les,
p
- am su - a - vis est, su - a - vis est. O - mni-
er barm-her - zig ist, barm-her - zig ist. Al - les,
p
est, quo - ni - am su - a - vis est. O - mni-
ist, weil er all - barm - her - zig ist. Al - les,

All things

28
mf
O - mni - a quae cun - que
Al - les, was sein Wil - le
p
O - mni - a quae cun - que vo - lu - it,
Al - les, was sein Wil - le frei er - dacht,
p
cresc.
O - mni - a quae cun - que vo - lu - it, fe - cit in
Al - les was sein Wil - le frei er - dacht, that er im
cresc.
-a quae cun - que vo - lu - it, o - mni - a, o - mni - a,
was sein Wil - le frei er - dacht, frei er - dacht, frei er - dacht,
cresc.
f
-a quae cun - que vo - lu - it. O - mni - a quae cun - que vo - lu it,
was sein Wil - le frei er - dacht. Al - les, was sein Wil - le frei er - dacht
cresc.
f
-a quae cun - que vo - lu - it. O - mni - a quae cun - que vo - lu -
was sein Wil - le frei er - dacht. Al - les, was sein Wil - le frei er -

whatever he wished,

he made, in heaven and on earth.

Praise the Lord, for his name is noble and sublime.

39
p
-mi - ni e - jus, quo - ni -
ist sein Na - me, weil er
p
- mi - ni e - jus, lau - da - te Do - mi -
- me hehr und gross, lob - prei - set Gott den
p
no - mi - ni e - jus, quo - ni - am su - a - vis
ist sein Na - me, weil er all - barm - her - zig
p
no - mi - ni e - jus, quo - ni - am su - a - vis
gross ist sein Na - me, weil er all - barm - her - zig
p
no - mi - ni e - jus, quo - ni - am su - a - vis
sein Na - me hehr und gross, weil er all - barm - her - zig
p
cresc.
- ni e - jus, lau - da - te Do - mi - num, lau -
Na - - - me, lob - prei - set Gott den Herrn, lob -

42
f
-am su - a - vis est, su - a - - vis
all - barm-her - zig ist, barm - her - - zig
f
-num, quo - ni - am su - a - vis est, quo -
Herrn, weil er all - barm-her - zig ist, weil
f
est, lau - da - te Do - mi -
ist, lob - prei - set Gott den
cresc.
f
est, quo - ni - am su - a - vis est, quo - ni -
ist, weil er all - barm - her-zig ist, weil er
f
est, quo - ni - am su - a - vis
ist, weil er all - barm - her - zig
f
- da - te Do - mi - num, quo - ni - am su -
- prei - set Gott den Herrn, weil er all - - barm -

45
est, lau-da-te Do - - mi - num, lau-da -
ist, lob-prei-set Gott den Herrn, lob-prei -
- ni - am su - a - vis est, lau-da -
er all - - barm-her - zig ist, lob-prei -
- num, lau-da - te, lau-da -
Herrn, lob - prei - set, lob - prei -
- am, su - a - vis est, su - a - vis est, lau-da -
all - barm-her - zig ist, barm - her - zig ist, lob-prei -
est, quo - ni - am su - a - vis est, su - a - vis
ist, weil er all - barm - her - zig ist, lob- prei -
- a - vis est, quo - ni - am su - a - - vis
- her - zig ist, weil er all - barm - her - - zig

48
ff
- te, lau - da - te, lau - da - te Do - mi - num.
- set, lob - prei - set, lob - prei - set Gott den Herrn.
- te, lau - da - te Do - - - mi - num.
- set, lob - prei - set Gott den Herrn.
- te, lau - da - te, lau - da - te Do - mi - num.
- set, lob - prei - set, lob - prei - set Gott den Herrn.
- te, lau - da - te Do - mi - num.
- set, lob - prei - set Gott den Herrn.
est, lau - da - te, lau - da - te Do - mi - num.
- set, lob - prei - set, lob - prei - set Gott den Herrn.
est, lau - da - te, lau - da - te Do - mi - num.
ist, lob - prei - set, lob - prei - set Gott den Herrn.

Meditabor
(Denken will ich)

Offertory for the 2nd Sunday in Lent

Josef Rheinberger (1839–1901)
4 Sechsstimmige Motetten, Op. 133, no. 2

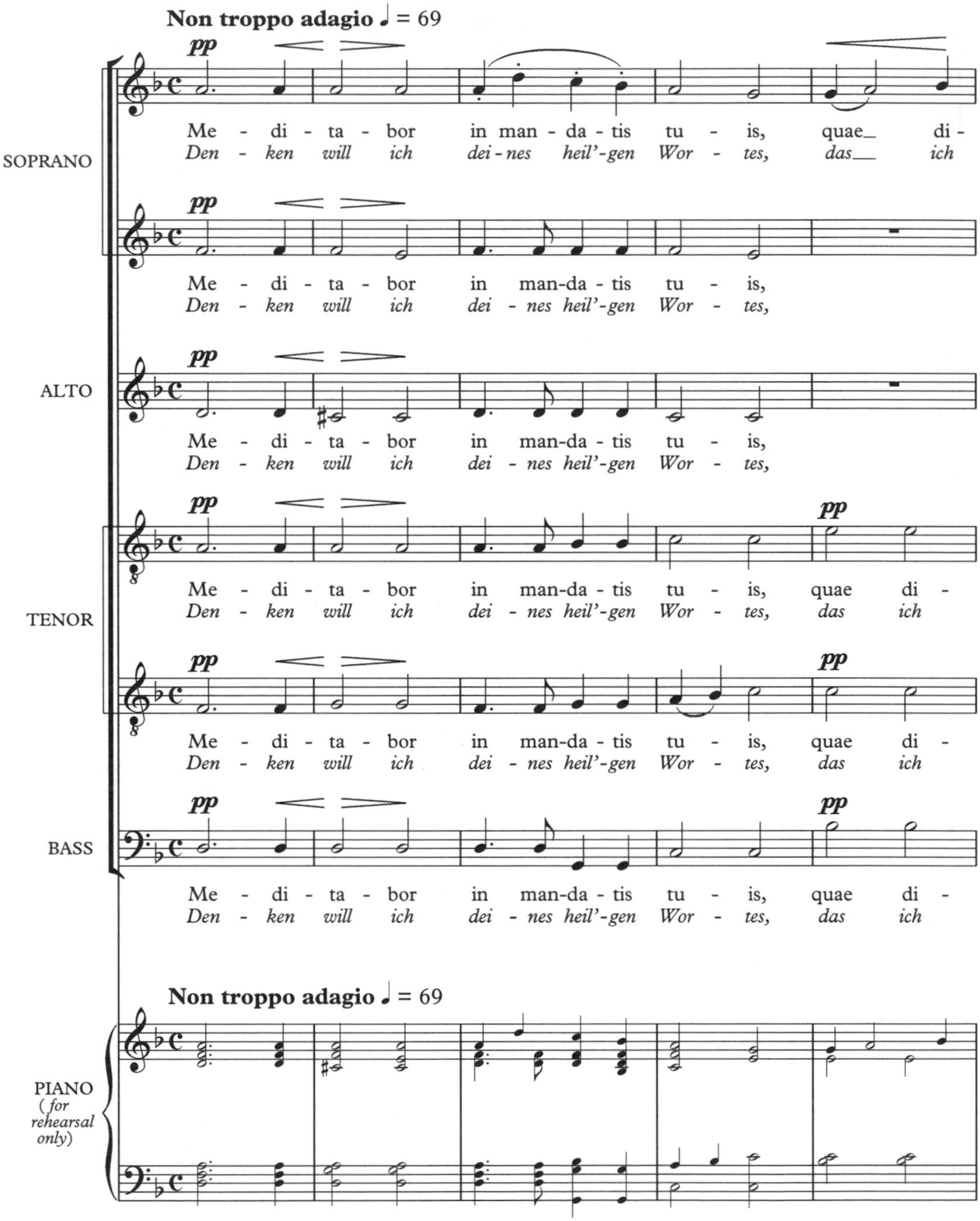

I will meditate on your commands which I

6
f
mf
-le - xi, val - de, val - - de, et le -
lie - be, wahr - haft lie - - be, und be -
quae_ di - le - xi, val - - de, et le -
das___ ich wahr - haft lie - - be, und be -
quae_ di - le - xi, val - - de, et le -
das___ ich wahr - haft lie - - be, und be -
-le - xi, quae_ di - le - xi, val - - de,
lie - be, das___ ich wahr - haft lie - - be,
-le - xi, quae di - le - xi, val - - de,
lie - be, das ich___ wahr - haft lie - - be,
-le - xi, quae di - le - xi, val - - de,
lie - be, das ich___ wahr - haft lie - - be,
love exceedingly;
I will

raise my hands to greet your commands

16
p
quae dile -
das ich lie -
p
cresc.
quae dile - xi, quae di-
das ich lie - be, das ich
p
mf
quae di - le - xi, quae
das ich lie - be, das
pp
me - as ad man - da - ta tu - a, quae di - le - xi,
Hän-de dein Ge - setz zu ü - ben, das ich lie - be,
pp
me - as ad man-da - ta tu - a, quae di - le - xi,
Hän - de dein Ge-setz zu ü - ben, das ich lie - be,
pp
me - as ad man-da - ta tu - a, quae di - le - xi,
Hän - de dein Ge-setz zu ü - ben, das ich lie - be,

which I love.

21
mf
-xi, me - di - ta - bor in man-da-tis tu - is,
-be, den - ken_ will ich dei-nes heil'-gen Wor - tes,
mf
-le - xi, me - di - ta - bor in man - da - tis,__
lie - be, den - ken_ will____ ich dei-nes Wor - tes,__
mf
__ di - le - xi, me - di - ta-bor in man - da -
__ ich lie - be, den - ken_ will ich dei-nes Wor -
mf
quae__ di - le - xi, val - de, quae_ di-
das___ ich lie - be, wahr - haft, wahr - haft
cresc.
quae di - le - xi, val - de,____ val - de,__ quae_ di-
das ich lie - be, wahr - haft____ lie - be,__ das_ ich
cresc.
quae di - le - xi, me - di - ta-bor in man-da-tis tu -
das ich lie - be, den - ken will ich dei-nes heil'-gen Wor -

26
f
p
quae di - le - xi val - de, quae___ di - le - xi val - de, et le -
das ich wahr-haft lie - be, das___ ich wahr-haft lie - be, und be -
quae di - le - xi val - de, quae___ di - le - xi val - de, et le -
das ich wahr-haft lie - be, das___ ich wahr-haft lie - be, und be -
- tis, quae di - le - xi et le - va - bo
- tes, das ich lie - be, und be - reit sind
- le - xi, quae___ di - le - xi val - de, quae___ di - le - xi, et le - va - bo
lie - be, das___ ich wahr-haft lie - be, das___ ich lie - be, und be - reit sind
- le - xi, quae___ di - le - xi val - de, quae___ di - le - xi, et le - va - bo
lie - be, das___ ich wahr - haft lie - be, das___ ich lie - be, und be - reit sind
- is, et le - va - bo
- tes, und be - reit sind

31
f
-va - bo ma - nus me - as,
-reit sind mei - ne Hän - de,
f
-va - bo ma - nus me - as,
-reit sind mei - ne Hän - de,
f
p dolce
ma - nus me - as, ma-nus me - as, ad man - da - ta
mei - ne Hän - de, mei-ne Hän - de, dein Ge - setz zu
f
ma - nus me - as, ma-nus me - as,
mei - ne Hän - de, mei-ne Hän - de,
f
ma - nus me - - - - - as,
mei - ne Hän - - - - de,
f
ma - nus me - as, ma-nus me - as,
mei - ne Hän - de, mei-ne Hän - de,

36
p dolce
ad man - da - ta tu - a, quae di -
dein Ge - setz zu ü - ben, das ich
p dolce
ad man - da - ta tu - a, quac di -
dein Ge - setz zu ü - ben, das ich
tu - a, quae di - le - xi val - de,
ü - ben, das ich wahr - haft lie - be,
p
ad man - da - ta tu - a, quae di -
dein Ge - setz zu ü - ben, das ich
p
ad man - da - ta tu - a, quae di -
dein Ge - setz zu ü - ben, das ich
p
ad man-da - ta tu - a, quae di -
dein Ge-setz zu ü - ben, das ich

41
mf
- le - xi val - de, me - - di -
wahr - haft lie - be, den - - ken
mf
- le - xi val - de, me - di -
wahr - haft lie - be, den - ken
mf cresc.
me - di - ta - - bor
den - ken will ich
mf cresc.
- le - xi val - de, me - di - ta - bor in man - da - tis,
wahr - haft lie - be, den - ken will ich dei - nes Wor - tes,
mf cresc.
- le - xi val - de, me - - - - - di - ta - bor,
wahr - haft lie - be, den - - - - - ken will ich,
mf
- le - xi val - de, me - di -
wahr - haft lie - be, den - ken

46
cresc.
f
ff
-ta - - bor, me - di - ta - - bor in man - da - tis
will ich, den - ken will ich dei - nes heil' - gen
f
ff
-ta - - bor in man - da - tis tu -
will ich dei - nes heil' - gen Wor -
cresc.
f
ff
me - di - ta - bor in man - da - - tis tu -
den - ken will ich dei - nes heil' - - gen Wor -
f
ff
me - di - ta - bor in man - da - tis tu -
den - ken will ich dei - nes heil'-gen Wor -
f
ff
me - di - ta - bor in man - da - tis tu - - is,
den - ken will ich dei - nes heil'-gen Wor - tes,
f
ff
-ta - bor in man - da - tis tu - - is,
will ich dei - nes heil' - gen Wor - tes,

51
pp
tu - is, quae di - le - - xi, quae di -
Wor - tes, das ich lie - - be, das ich
pp
- is, quae di - le - - xi, quae di -
- tes, das ich lie - - be, das ich
pp
- is, quae di - le - - xi, quae di -
- tes, das ich lie - - be, das ich
pp dolce
- is, quae di - le - xi, quae di - le - xi,
- tes, das ich lei - be, das ich lie - be,
quae di - le - xi, di - le - xi,
das ich lie - be, ich lie - be,
quae di - le - - - - - xi,
das ich lie - - - - - be,

56
pp
-le - xi, quae di - le - xi val - - - de.
lie - be, das ich wahr - haft lie - - - be.
pp
-le - xi, quae di - le - xi val - - - de.
lie - be, das ich wahr - haft lie - - - be.
pp
-le - xi, quae di - le - xi val - de, val - de.
lie - be, das ich wahr - haft, wahr - haft lie - be.
pp
quae di - le - xi, di - le - xi val - de, val - de.
das ich lie - be, ich wahr - haft, wahr - haft lie - be.
pp
f
pp
quae di - le - xi, quae di - le - xi val - de.
das ich lie - be, das ich wahr - haft lie - be.
pp
f
pp
quae di - le - xi, quae di - le - xi val - de.
das ich lie - be, das ich wahr - haft lie - be.

Morgenlied

August Heinrich Hoffmann von Fallersleben
(1798–1874)

Josef Rheinberger (1839–1901)
Drei geistliche Gesänge, Op. 69, no. 1

The stars have faded with their golden glow,

5
ih - rem güld - nen Schein, bald ist die Nacht ent - wi - chen, der
ih - rem güld - nen Schein, bald ist die Nacht ent - wi - chen, der
ih - rem güld - nen Schein, bald ist die Nacht ent - wi - chen, der
ih - rem güld - nen Schein, bald ist die Nacht ent - wi - chen, der
ih - rem güld - nen Schein, der
ih - rem güld - nen Schein, der
soon the night will be past, the
9
Mor - gen dringt her - ein, der Mor - gen dringt her - ein. Noch
Mor - gen dringt her - ein, dringt her - ein.
Mor - gen dringt her - ein, der Mor - gen dringt her - ein.
Mor - gen dringt her - ein, der Mor - gen dringt her - ein. Noch
Mor - gen dringt her - ein, der Mor - gen dringt her - ein.
Mor - gen dringt her - ein, der Mor - gen dringt her - ein. Noch
morning dawns. Now

13
wal - tet tie - fes Schwei - gen im Tal,
p
Noch wal - tet tie - fes_ Schwei-gen im Tal und ü - ber-
p
Noch wal - tet tie - fes_ Schwei-gen im Tal und ü - ber-
wal - tet tie - fes Schwei - gen im Tal, im
p
Noch wal - tet tie - fes Schwei - gen im Tal_ und_ ü - ber -
wal - tet tie - fes Schwei-gen, noch wal - tet tie - fes Schwei - gen im
a deep silence swirls in the valley,
and everywhere.
17
f
im Tal und_ ü - ber - all. Auf frisch - be - tau - ten
p
- all, im Tal und ü - ber - all. Auf frisch - be-tau - ten
f
p
- all, im_ Tal und ü - ber - all. Auf frisch - be-tau - ten
f
p
Tal, im Tal_ und_ ü - ber - all.
f
- all, im Tal und ü - ber - all.
f
Tal und ü - ber - all.
f
On branches fresh

21
Zwei-gen singt nur die Nach-ti-gall,
Zwei - gen singt nur die Nach-ti - gall, singt nur die Nach - ti-gall,
Zwei - gen singt nur die Nach-ti - gall, singt nur die
Auf frisch be - tau - ten Zwei - gen
Auf frisch be - tau - ten Zwei - gen
Auf frisch be - tau - ten Zwei - gen
with dew, only the nightingale sings.
26
singt nur die Nach - ti-gall, singt nur, singt nur die Nach - ti -
singt nur, singt nur die Nach - ti -
Nach - ti-gall, singt nur, singt nur die Nach - ti -
singt nur die Nach - ti - gall, singt nur die Nach - ti -
singt nur die Nach - ti - gall, singt nur die Nach - ti -
singt nur die Nach - ti - gall, singt nur die Nach - ti -

She sings praise and

40
Lob und Eh - re, sie sin - get Lob und Eh -
Sie sin - get Lob und Eh - re, sie sin - get
Lob und Eh - re, und Eh - re, und Eh - re, sie sin -
Eh - re, sie sin - get Lob und Eh - re,
Eh - re, sie sin - get Lob, Lob und Eh - re, sie
Lob und Eh - re, und Eh - re, sie sin - get Lob, Eh -
honour,
44
- re, sie sin - get Lob dem ho - hen Herrn,
Lob und Eh - re, sie sin - get Lob dem ho - hen Herrn,
-get Lob, Eh - re, sie sin - get Lob dem ho - hen Herrn,
sie sin - get Lob und Eh - re dem ho - hen Herrn,
sin - get Lob, Eh - re, sie singt dem ho - hen Herrn,
- re, sie sin - get Lob, Eh - re dem ho - hen Herrn, dem ho - hen
she sings to the highest Lord

48
— dem ho - hen Herrn der Welt, dem ho - hen Herrn der
— dem Herrn der Welt, dem ho - hen Herrn der
— dem ho - hen Herrn der Welt, dem ho - hen Herrn der
— dem ho - hen Herrn der Welt, dem ho - hen Herrn der
— dem ho - hen Herrn der Welt, dem ho - hen Herrn der
Herrn, dem Herrn der Welt, dem Herrn der
p
dim.
in the world,
52
Welt, der ü-ber'm Land, der ü-ber'm Mee - re
Welt, der ü-ber'm Land, der ü-ber'm Mee - re die Hand des
Welt, der ü - ber'm Land, ü - ber'm Mee - re
Welt,
Welt, der ü - ber'm Land und Mee - re
Welt, der ü-ber'm Land, der ü-ber'm
mf
who over the earth,
over the oceans,

holds his hand of blessing.

67
ü - ber'm Land und Mee - re die Hand des Se - gens
pp
die Hand des Se - gens
ü - ber'm Land und Mee - re die Hand des Se - gens
pp
der ü - ber'm Land die Hand des Se - - gens
Land und ü - ber'm Mee - re die Hand des Se - gens
73
hält.
f
Er hat die Nacht ver -
hält.
f
Er hat die Nacht ver -
hält.
f
Er hat die Nacht ver -
hält.
mf
f
Er hat die Nacht ver - trie - ben, ihr Kind-lein fürch - tet
hält.
mf
f
Er hat die Nacht ver - trie - ben, ihr Kind-lein fürch - tet
mf
f
Er hat die Nacht ver - trie - ben, ihr Kind - lein fürch - tet
He has driven away the night,
you little children need fear

78
- trie - ben, ihr Kind - lein fürch - tet nichts; stets kommt zu sei - nen
- trie - ben, ihr Kind - lein fürch - tet nichts; stets kommt zu sei - nen
- trie - ben, ihr Kind - lein fürch - tet nichts; stets kommt zu sei - nen
nichts, ihr Kind - lein fürch - tet nichts; stets kommt zu sei - nen
nichts, ihr Kind - lein fürch - tet nichts;
nichts, ihr Kind - lein fürch - tet nichts;
nothing;
always comes to his
82
Lie - ben der Va - ter al - les Lichts, der Va - ter al - les
Lie - ben der Va - ter al - les Lichts, al - les
Lie - ben der Va - ter al - les Lichts, der Va - ter al - les
Lie - ben der Va - ter al - les Lichts, der Va - ter al - les
der Va - ter al - les Lichts, der Va - ter al - les
der Va - ter al - les Lichts, der Va - ter al - les
loved ones the father of all light.

86
p
cresc.
Lichts, er hat die Nacht ver - trie - ben, ihr Kind - lein fürch-tet nichts, er
Lichts, er hat die Nacht ver - trie - ben, ihr Kind - lein fürch-tet nichts, er
Lichts, er hat die Nacht ver - trie - ben, ihr Kind - lein fürch-tet nichts, er
Lichts, er hat die Nacht ver - trie - ben, ihr Kind - lein fürch-tet nichts, er
Lichts, er hat die Nacht ver - trie - ben, ihr Kind - lein fürch-tet nichts, er
Lichts, er hat die Nacht ver - trie - ben, ihr Kind - lein fürch-tet nichts, er
91
ff
hat die Nacht ver - trie - ben, ihr Kind - lein fürch - tet nichts, stets
hat die Nacht ver - trie - ben, ihr Kind - lein fürch - tet nichts, stets
hat die Nacht ver - trie - ben, ihr Kind - lein fürch - tet nichts, stets kommt
hat die Nacht ver - trie - ben, ihr Kind - lein fürch - tet nichts, stets
hat die Nacht ver - trie - ben, ihr Kind - lein fürch - tet nichts, stets kommt
hat die Nacht ver - trie - ben, ihr Kind - lein fürch - tet nichts, stets

95
kommt zu sei - nen Lie - ben der Va - ter, der Va - ter,
kommt zu sei - nen Lie - ben der Va - ter al - les Lichts,
zu sei - nen Lie - ben der Va - ter al - les Lichts, der
kommt zu sei - nen Lie - ben der Va - ter, der Va - ter al - les Lichts, der
zu sei - nen Lie - ben der Va - ter, der Va - ter al - les Lichts, der
kommt zu sei - nen Lie - ben der Va - ter, der Va - ter al - les Lichts, der
100
der Va - ter al - les, al - - les Lichts.
der Va - ter al - les, al - - les Lichts.
Va - ter al - les Lichts, der Va - ter al - - les Lichts.
Va - ter al - les Lichts, der Va - ter al - - les Lichts.
Va - ter al - les Lichts, al - les, al - - les Lichts.
Va - ter al - les Lichts, al - les, al - - les Lichts.
p
ff
dim.

Tribulationes
(Leiden und Bedrängnis)

Psalm 25, vv. 17–18

Josef Rheinberger (1839–1901)
5 Hymnen, Op. 140, no. 1

10
f
di-la - ta - tae sunt: de ne-
sie ver - mehr - ten sich: aus der
f
di-la - ta - - - tae_ sunt: de ne-
sie ver - mehr - - - ten_ sich: aus der
f
sunt,_ di - - la - ta - tae sunt: de ne-
sich,_ sie_ ver - mehr - ten sich: aus der
cresc.
f
-ta - tae sunt,_ di - la - ta - tae sunt: de ne-
-mehr - ten sich,_ sie ver - mehr - ten sich: aus der
from my
15
p
-ces - si-ta - ti-bus me - is e - ri - pe me, Do-mi-ne.
Noth und Drang - sal des Le - bens ret - te mich, du Gott und Herr.
-ces - si-ta - ti-bus me - is e - ri - pe me, Do-mi-ne.
Noth und Drang - sal des Le - bens ret - te mich, du Gott und Herr.
-ces - si-ta - ti-bus me - is e - ri - pe me, Do-mi-ne.
Noth und Drang - sal des Le - bens ret - te mich, du Gott und Herr.
-ces - si-ta - ti-bus me - is e - ri - pe me, Do-mi-ne.
Noth und Drang - sal des Le - bens ret - te mich, du Gott und Herr.
needs, save me, Lord.

20
p cresc.
Vi - de hu - mi - li - ta - tem me - am et la-
Sieh', wie mein Herz Ver - za - gen fül - let, sieh' die
Vi - de hu - mi - li - ta - tem_ me - am et la-
Sieh', wie mein Herz Ver - za - gen_ fül - let, sieh' die
Vi - de, Vi - de hu - mi - li - ta - tem me - am et la-
Sie - he, Sieh', wie mein Herz_ Ver - za - gen fül - let, sieh' die
Vi - de hu - mi - li - ta - tem me - am
Sieh', wie mein Herz_ Ver - za - gen fül - let,
See my humility
and
25
cresc.
f
-bo - rem me - um, et la - bo - rem me - um, et di - mit - te
schwe - ren Käm - pfe, sieh' die schwe - ren Käm - pfe, und ver - gieb_ mir
-bo - rem me - um, et la - bo - rem me - um, et di - mit - te_
schwe - ren Käm - pfe, sieh' die schwe - ren Käm - pfe, und ver - gieb_ mir_
-bo - rem me - um, la - bo - rem_ me - um, et di - mit - te
schwe - ren Käm - pfe, die schwe - ren_ Käm - pfe, und ver - gieb,_ ver -
et la - bo - rem me - um, et di - mit - te, di - mit - te
sieh' die schwe - ren Käm - pfe, und ver - gieb mir, ver - gieb_ mir
mf
my hardship
and dismiss

30
om - ni - a pec - ca - ta me - a.
je - de Schuld, jeg - li - che Tor - heit.
om - ni - a pec - ca - ta me - a.
je - de Schuld, jeg - li - che Tor - heit.
p dolce
om - ni - a pec - ca - ta me - a. Vi -
gieb mir je - de Schuld und Tor - heit. Sieh',
om - ni - a pec - ca - ta me - a.
je - de Schuld und je - de Tor - heit.
p
all my sins.
35
p dolce
p
cresc.
Vi - de hu - mi - li - ta - tem me - am, et la - bo - rem
Sieh', wie mein Herz Ver - za - gen fül - let, sieh' die schwe - ren
Vi - de hu - mi - li - ta - tem me - am, et la - bo - rem
Sieh', wie mein Herz Ver - za - gen fül - let, sieh' die schwe - ren
- de hu - mi - li - ta - tem me - am, et la - bo - rem
wie mein Herz Ver - za - gen fül - let, sieh' die schwe - ren
Vi - de hu - mi - li - ta - tem me - am, et la - bo - rem
Sieh', wie mein Herz Ver - za - gen fül - let, sieh' die schwe - ren
mf

40
me - um, et di - mit - te om-ni - a pec - ca - ta me - a.
Käm - pfe, und ver - gieb___ mir je - de Schuld und je - de Tor - heit.
me - um, et di - mit - te om - ni - a pec - ca - ta me - a.
Käm - pfe, und ver - gieb mir je - de Schuld und je - de Tor - heit.
me - um, et di - mit - te om-ni - a pec - ca - ta me - a.
Käm - pfe, und ver - gieb___ mir je - de Schuld und je - de Tor - heit.
me - um, et di - mit - te om - ni - a pec - ca - ta me - a.
Käm - pfe, und ver - gieb mir je - de Schuld und je - de Tor - heit.
45
Tri - bu - la - ti-
Lei - den und Be-
Tri - bu - la - ti-
Lei - den und Be-
Tri - bu - la - ti-
Lei - den und Be-
Tri - bu - la - ti -
Lei - den und Be -

50
sf p
-o - nes cor - dis me - i
-dräng - niss mei - ner See - le
sf p f
-o - nes cor - dis me - i di - la -
-dräng - niss mei - ner See - le sie ver-
sf p mf cresc.
-o - nes cor - dis me - i di - la - ta - tae
-dräng - niss mei - ner See - le sie ver - mehr - ten
sf p mf cresc.
-o - nes cor - dis me - i di - la - ta - tae sunt, di - la -
-dräng - niss mei - ner See - le sie ver - mehr - ten sich, sie ver -
mf
55
f pp cresc.
di - la - ta - tae sunt, de ne - ces - si - ta - ti - bus
sie ver - mehr - ten sich, von des Le - bens Not und Drang -
pp cresc.
- ta - tae sunt, de ne - ces - si - ta - ti - bus
-mehr - ten sich, von des Le - bens Not und Drang -
pp cresc.
sunt, di - la - ta - tae sunt, de ne - ces - si - ta - ti - bus
sich, sie ver - mehr - ten sich, von des Le - bens Not und Drang -
dim. p cresc.
- ta - tae sunt, de ne - ces - si -
-mehr - ten sich, von des Le - bens
pp cresc.

59
me - is e - ri - pe me, Do - mi - ne, e - ri - pe
- sal er - ret - te mich, o Gott und Herr, er - ret - te
me - is e - ri - pe me, Do - mi - ne,
- sal er - ret - te mich, o Gott und Herr,
me - is e - ri - pe me, Do - mi - ne, e - ri - pe
- sal er - ret - te mich, o Gott und Herr, er - ret - te mich,
- ta - ti - bus e - ri - pe me, Do - mi - ne, e -
Not und Drang - sal er - ret - te mich, o Herr, er - ret -
mf
64
rit.
dim.
me, Do - mi - ne.
mich, o Gott und Herr.
Do - mi - ne.
o Gott und Herr.
me, Do - mi - ne.
o Gott und Herr.
- ri - pe me, Do - mi - ne.
- te mich, o Gott und Herr.
p

An die Musik

adapted from the solo song, D. 547

Franz von Schober (1796–1882)

Franz Schubert (1797–1828)
arr. Lydia Smallwood

8
Le - bens wil - der Kreis um - strickt,
hei - li - ger Ak - kord von dir,
Hast du mein
Den Him - mel
Le - bens wil - der Kreis um - strickt,
hei - li - ger Ak - kord von dir,
Hast du mein
Den Him - mel
Le - bens wil - der Kreis um - strickt, Hast du mein Herz, mein
hei - li - ger Ak - kord von dir, Den Him - mel, den Him - mel
Le - bens wil - der Kreis um - strickt, Hast du mein Herz, mein
hei - li - ger Ak - kord von dir, Den Him - mel, den Him - mel
life's wild tumult,
chord from you
Have you kindled my
Has opened up a heaven
12
cresc.
Herz zu war - mer Lieb' ent - zun - den, Hast mich in ei - ne
bess' - rer Zei - ten mir er - schlos - sen, Du hol - de Kunst, ich
Herz zu war - mer Lieb' ent - zun - den, Hast mich in ei - ne
bess' - rer Zei - ten mir er - schlos - sen, Du hol - de Kunst, ich
Herz zu war - mer Lieb' ent - zun - den, Hast mich in ei - ne
bess' - rer Zei - ten mir er - schlos - sen, Du hol - de Kunst, ich
Herz zu war - mer, war - mer Lieb' ent - zun - den, Hast mich in
bess' - rer, bess' - rer Zei - ten mir er - schlos - sen, Du hol - de
heart to a warmer love,
of happier times,
Have you transported me
You lovely art, I

16
dim.
bess' - re Welt ent - rückt, in ei - ne bess' - re Welt ent - rückt!
dan - ke dir da - für, du hol - de Kunst, ich dan - ke dir!
dim.
bess' - re Welt ent - rückt, ei - ne bess' - re Welt ent - rückt!
dan - ke dir da - für, du Kunst, ich dan - ke dir!
dim.
bess' - re Welt ent - rückt, ei - ne bess' - re Welt ent - rückt!
dan - ke dir da - für, du Kunst, ich dan - ke dir!
dim.
ei - ne bess' - re Welt ent - rückt!
Kunst, ich dan - ke, dan - ke dir!
p

into a better world!
thank you for this!

20
fp
fp

Litanei auf das Fest Allerseelen

adapted from the solo song, D. 343

Johann Georg Jacobi (1740–1814)

Franz Schubert (1797–1828)
arr. Ralph Allwood

5
bang - es Quä-len, Die voll-en-det süs - sen Traum,
nicht zu zäh-len, Die ein fal-scher Freund ver-liess,
Dor - nen wach-ten, Gott, im rei-nen Him-mels-licht,
bang - es Quä-len, Die voll - en-det süs-sen Traum,
nicht zu zäh-len, Die ein fal-scher Freund ver - liess,
Dor - nen wach-ten, Gott, im rei-nen Him-mels - licht,
bang - es Quä-len, Die voll - en-det süs-sen Traum,
nicht zu zäh-len, Die ein fal-scher Freund ver - liess,
Dor - nen wach-ten, Gott, im rei-nen Him-mels - licht,
bang - es Quä-len, Die voll - en-det süs-sen Traum,
nicht zu zäh-len, Die ein fal-scher Freund ver - liess,
Dor - nen wach-ten, Gott, im rei-nen Him-mels - licht,
7
Le - bens-satt, ge-bo - ren kaum, Aus der Welt hin-ü - ber schie-den:
Und die blin - de Welt ver-stiess: Al - le, die von hin-nen schie-den:
Einst zu sehn vom An - ge-sicht: Al - le, die von hin-nen schie-den:
Le-bens - satt, ge - bo-ren kaum, Aus der Welt hin - ü - ber schie-den:
Und die blin - de Welt ver - stiess: Al - le, die von hin-nen schie-den:
Einst zu sehn vom An - ge - sicht: Al - le, die von hin-nen schie-den:
Le-bens - satt, ge - bo-ren kaum, Aus der Welt hin - ü - ber schie-den:
Und die blin - de Welt ver - stiess: Al - le, die von hin-nen schie-den:
Einst zu sehn vom An - ge - sicht: Al - le, die von hin-nen schie-den:
Le-bens - satt, ge - bo-ren kaum, Aus der Welt hin - ü - ber schie-den:
Und die blin - de Welt ver - stiess: Al - le, die von hin-nen schie-den:
Einst zu sehn vom An - ge - sicht: Al - le, die von hin-nen schie-den:
p

1. *Rest in peace all souls,*
Those who have finished with anxious torment,
Those whose sweet dreams are over,
Sated with life, hardly born,
From the world departed:
Rest in peace all souls!

2. *Loving maiden souls*
Whose tears cannot be counted
Who, abandoned by a false friend,
And disowned by a blind world:
All who have departed from this life,
Rest in peace all souls!

3. *And those who never enjoyed the sun,*
Lay awake under the moon on thorn bushes,
To see God, in the pure light of heaven
Once face to face:
All who have departed from this life,
Rest in peace all souls!

Zum Sanctus

from the Deutsche Messe, D. 872

Johann Philipp Neumann (1774–1849)

Franz Schubert (1797–1828)

An Webers Grabe

Richard Wagner

Richard Wagner (1813–83)
WWV 72

7
Hoch - ge-fühls, das uns-re Brust be-wegt! Nicht trau-ert mehr die
Hoch - ge - fühls, das uns-re Brust be - wegt! Nicht trau-ert mehr die
which move our breast!
No longer does
10
deut-sche Mut-ter Er - de um den ge-lieb - ten, weit ent-rück-ten Sohn;
German mother earth mourn for her beloved son, far away,

she no longer gazes with longing gestures over the ocean, to

far-off Albion: once more she has taken him back into her bosom, whom once she

20
f
p
aus-sandt' e - del, rein und gross. Hier, wo der Trau-er stum-me
aus - sandt' e - del, rein und gross. Hier, wo der
aus - sandt' e - del, rein und gross. Hier, wo der
aus - sandt' rein und gross. Hier, wo der
sent out, noble, pure and great.
Here, where the silent

24
f
Zäh - ren flos-sen, wo Lie-be noch das Teu-er-ste be-weint,–
Trau-er Zäh-ren flos-sen, wo Lieb' um den Teu - ren weint,– hier ward von
Trau-er Zäh-ren flos-sen, wo Lieb' um den Teu - ren weint,– hier ward von
Trau-er Zäh-ren flos-sen, wo Lieb' um den Teu - ren weint,–
tears of mourning flow,
where love still weeps over its dearest friend,
here

a noble league was founded by us, which unites us around him,

the marvellous one; here remains a true comrade of the league,

33
dim.
-nos - sen, hier grüs-set euch als from-me Pil - ger-
Bun-des Treu-ge-nos-sen, hier grüs-set euch als from - me
Bun-des Treu-ge-nos-sen, hier grüs-set euch als from - me
Bun-des Treu-ge-nos-sen, hier grüs - set euch als
here we greet you as a devout
36
- schar,– die schön - sten Blü - ten, die dem
Pil - ger - schar,– die schön-sten Blü - - ten,
Pil - ger - schar,– die schön-sten Blü - - ten,
from-me Pil - ger-schar,– die Blü - - ten,
band of pilgrims,
the most beautiful blooms

38
Bund ent - spros - sen, bringt op - - fernd die - ser
die dem Bund ent - spros - sen, bringt op - fernd die - ser
die dem Bund ent - spros - sen, bringt die - ser
die dem Bund ent - spros - sen, bringt op - fernd die - ser
which flower from the league, we offer in sacrifice
40
dim.
ed - len Stät - te dar! Denn hier ruh' Er, be -
ed - len Stät - te dar! Denn hier ruh' Er, be -
ed - len Stät - te dar! Denn hier ruh' Er, be -
ed - len Stät - te dar! Denn hier ruh'
at this noble place! For here he rests,

admired and beloved, who gives the solemn blessing to our league.

Aufblick

Joseph von Eichendorff (1788–1857)

Hugo Wolf (1839–1901)
6 geistliche Lieder, no. 1

7
- ü - ber-wind-lich, bin ich mit dir! Herr, im Ge-tüm - mel
un - ü - ber-wind - lich, bin ich mit dir! Herr, im Ge-tüm - mel
invincible, I am with you!
10
zeig' dein Pa-nier! Un - ü - ber-wind - lich bin ich mit dir!

Ergebung

Joseph von Eichendorff (1788–1857)
from *Der Pilger*

Hugo Wolf (1839–1901)
6 geistliche Lieder, no. 5

Ziemlich gehalten [♩ = 84]
SOPRANO
ALTO
TENOR
BASS
PIANO (for rehearsal only)
Dein Wil - le, Herr, ge - sche - he! Ver - dun - kelt schweigt das Land.
Dein Wil - le, Herr, ge - sche - he! Ver - dun - kelt schweigt das Land.
Im Zug der Wet - ter
Im Zug der Wet - ter seh',
May you will, Lord, be done!
Darkened,
the land is silent.
Through the weather,

I see, trembling, your hand.

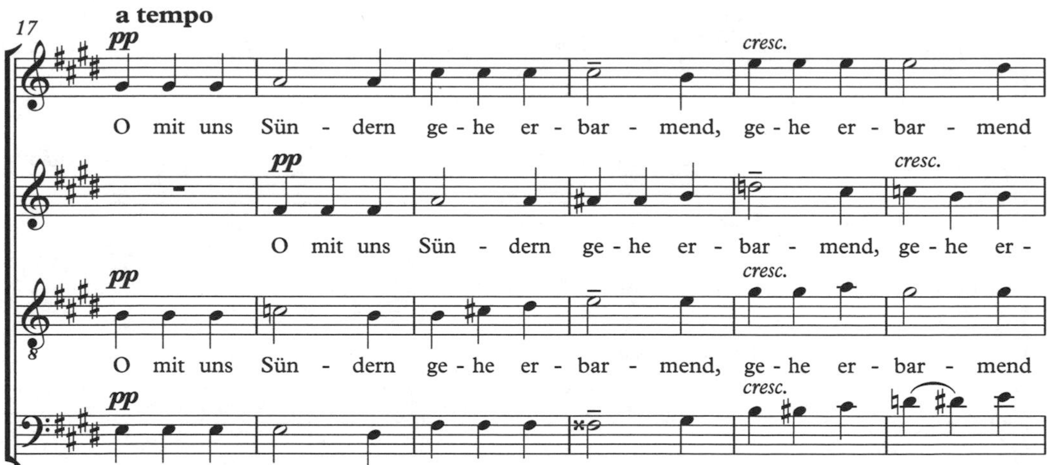

O with us sinners be merciful

23
ins Ge - richt! Ich beug' im tief - sten We - he, im
-bar - mend ins Ge - richt! Ich beug' im tief - sten
ins Ge - richt! Ich beug' im Weh', im tief - sten
ins Ge - richt! Ich beug' im tief - sten We - he, im
in judgment
I bow in deepest sorrow,
28
rit.
dim.
p dim.
tief - sten We - he zum Staub mein An - ge - sicht.
We - he, im tief - sten We - he zum Staub mein An - ge - sicht.
Weh' zum Staub, zum Staub mein An - ge - sicht.
tief - sten We - he zum Staub mein An - ge - sicht.
my face to the dust.

May your will, Lord, be done!

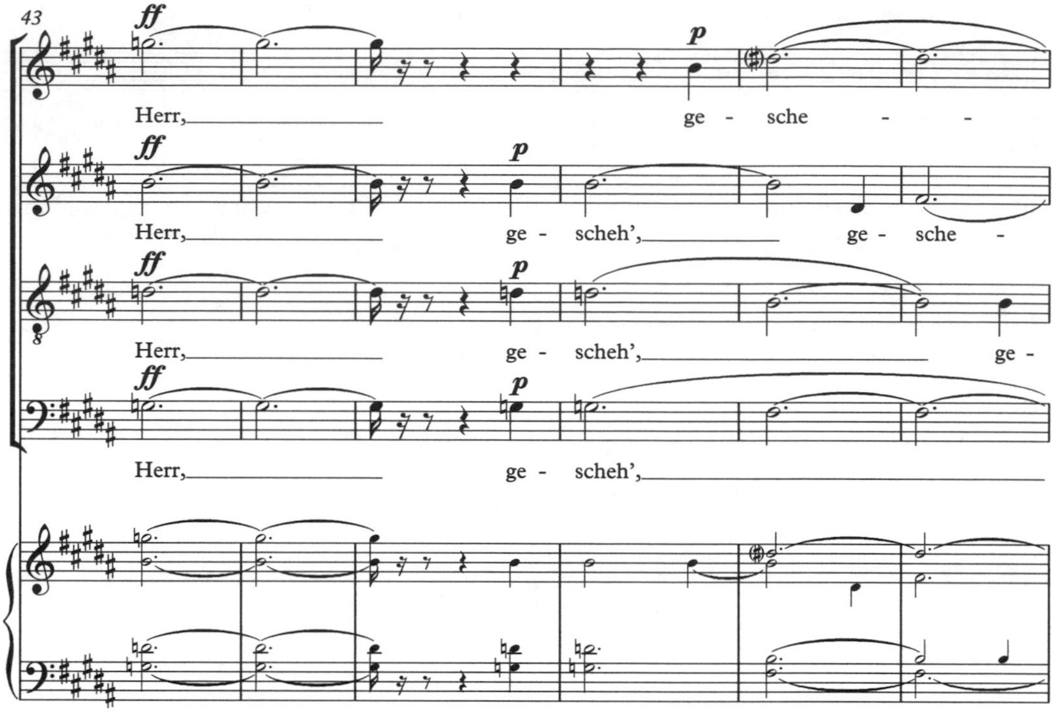
43
ff
p
Herr, ge - sche - -
Herr, ge - scheh', ge - sche -
Herr, ge - scheh', ge -
Herr, ge - scheh',

49
più p
- - - he, gesheh',
- - - he, er ge - sche - he,
- sche - - he, er ge - sche - he,
ge - sche - he, er ge - sche - he,

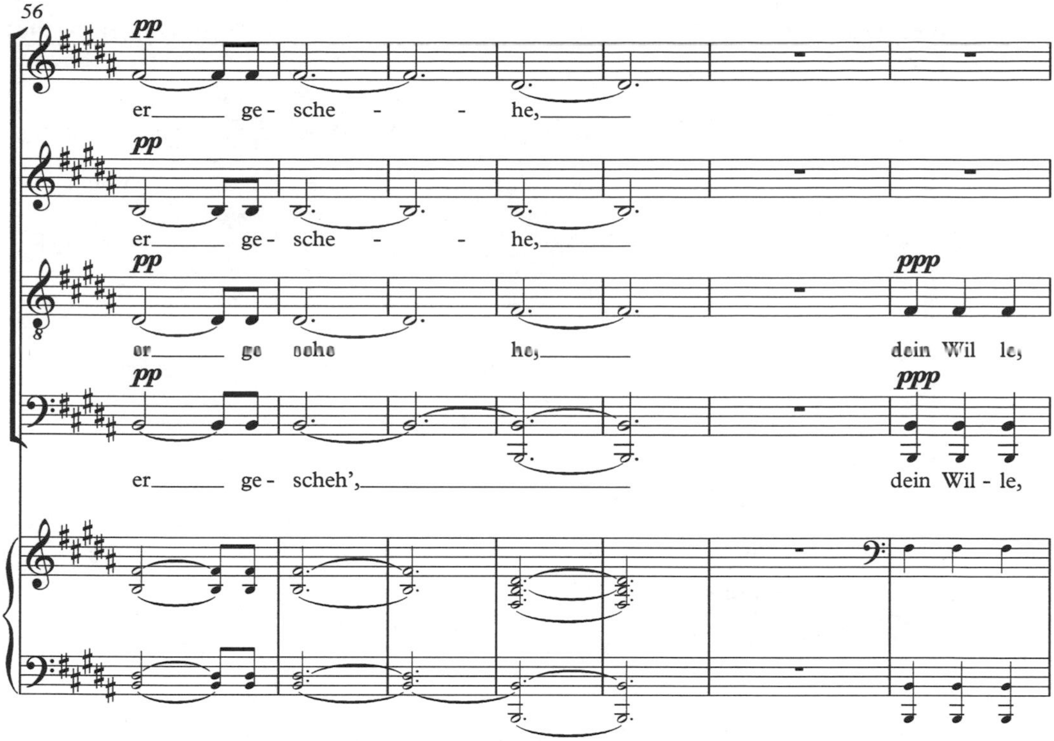
56
pp
er ge - sche - - he,
pp
er ge - sche - - he,
pp
er ge - sche he,
ppp
dein Wil le,
pp
er ge - scheh',
ppp
dein Wil - le,

63
ppp
er ge - sche - - he!
ppp
er ge - sche - - he!
Herr, ge - sche - - - - - - he!
Herr, ge - sche - - - - - - he!

Letzte Bitte

Joseph von Eichendorff (1788–1857)
from *Der Pilger*

Hugo Wolf (1839–1901)
6 geistliche Lieder, no. 4

Like a mortally wounded champion, who has lost his way,

I now waver and can go no further, by life

weary for death. *Night already protects all the tired,*

and it is so still around me. *Lord, also give peace finally to me,*

for I wish and hope no more!

1 2 3 4 5 6 7 8 9

Texts

Abendlied

August H. Plinke
Max Reger, *Drei sechsstimmige Chöre*, Op. 39, no. 2, 1899

Leise geht der Tag zur Rüste;
purpurrot zum letztenmal glüht der Wald,
als ob ihn küsste heiß der Sonne goldner Strahl.
Weiße Nebelschleier steigen wallend aus dem See empor.
Rings ist Stille nur und Schweigen,
Stille und kein Laut klingt an mein Ohr.
Und es streben alle müden Seelen nun der Heimat zu.
Denn der Abend lockt mit Frieden und die Nacht mit süßer Ruh.
Und in ferne Weltenweiten wogt die Seele mir hinaus,
gleich als wollte sie bereiten sich zum ew'gen Flug ins Vaterhaus.

O Tod, wie bitter bist du

German by Martin Luther (1483-1546): Ecclesiasticus, ch. 41, vv. 1-2
Max Reger, *Geistliche Gesänge*, Op. 110, no. 3, 1912

O Tod, wie bitter bist du, wenn an dich gedenket ein Mensch, der gute Tage und genug hat, und ohne Sorgen lebet; und dem es wohl geht in allen Dingen und wohl noch essen mag! O Tod, wie wohl tust du dem Dürftigen, der da schwach und alt ist, der in allen Sorgen steckt und nichts Bessers zu hoffen noch zu erwarten hat.

Abendlied

Luke ch. 24, v. 29
Josef Rheinberger, *Drei geistliche Gesänge*, Op. 69, no. 3

Bleib bei uns, denn es will Abend werden, und der Tag hat sich geneiget.

Anima nostra (Unsere Seele)

Offertory for the Feast of the Innocents, 28 December
Josef Rheinberger, *4 Sechsstimmige Motetten*, Op. 133, no. 1, 1883

Anima nostra, sicut passer, erepta est de laqueo vernantium. Laqueus contritus est, et nos liberati sumus. Adjutorium nostrum in nomine Domini, qui fecit coelum et terram. Alleluja.

[text also given in the motet in German]

Unsere Seele, gleich dem Sperling ward sie befreit, vom Pfeil des Feind's, der sie verfolgt. Das Geschoß ist abgestumpft, vom Feinde sind wir errettet. Jedem Bangen der Erde wird Hilfe von Gott allein; er schuf den Himmel, schuf Alles. Alleluja.

Eripe me (Rette mich, Herr)

Psalm 142, v. 11
Josef Rheinberger, *5 Hymnen*, Op. 140, no. 3, 1884

Eripe me de inimicis meis, Domine! Ad te confugi, doce me facere voluntatem tuam. Eripe me, quia Deus meus es tu.

[text also given in the motet in German]

Rette mich, Herr, vom Feinde meiner Seele, rette mich, Gott und Herr! Zu dir entflieh' ich, helfe mir, lehre mich dein Gesetz zu halten. Denn du bist mein Schöpfer und Gott!

Laudate Dominum (Lobpreiset Gott den Herrn)

Psalm 134, vv. 3, 6
Josef Rheinberger, *4 Sechsstimmige Motetten*, Op. 133, no. 3

Laudate Dominum quia benignus est, psallite nomini ejus. Laudate Dominum quoniam suavis est. Omnia quae cunque voluit, fecit in coelo, et in terra.

[text also given in the motet in German]

Lobpreiset Gott den Herrn, weil er barmherzig ist, und groß und herrlich sein Name. Alles, was sein Wille frei erdacht, that er im Himmel und auf Erden, lobpreiset Gott den Herrn, denn groß und hehr ist sein Name.

Morgenlied

August Heinrich Hoffmann von Fallersleben (1798-1874)
Josef Rheinberger, *Drei geistliche Gesänge*, Op. 69, No. 1

Die Sterne sind erblichen mit ihrem güldnen Schein,
bald ist die Nacht entwichen, der Morgen dringt herein.
Noch wallet tiefes Schweigen im Tal, und überall,
Auf frischbetauten Zweigen singt nur die Nachtigall.
Sie singet Lob und Ehre, dem hohen Herrn der Welt,
der über'm Land, der über'm Meere die Hand des Segens hält.
Er hat die Nacht vertrieben, ihr Kindlein fürchtet nichts;
stets kommt zu seinen Lieben der Vater alles Lichts.

Meditabor (Denken will ich)

Offertory for the 2nd Sunday in Lent
Josef Rheinberger, *4 Sechsstimmige Motetten*, Op. 133, no. 2

Meditabor in mandatis tuis, quae dilexi valde et levabo manus meas
ad mandata tua, quae dilexi.

[text also given in the motet in German]

Denken will ich deines heil'gen Wortes, das ich liebe, das ich wahrhaft
liebe, und befreit sind meine Hände dein Gesetz zu üben.

Tribulationes (Leiden und Bedrängnis)

Psalm 25, vv. 17-18
Josef Rheinberger, *5 Hymnen*, Op. 140, no. 1, 1884

Tribulationes cordis mei dilatatae sunt: de necessitatibus meis
eripe me, Domine. Vide humilitatem meum et laborem meum, et
dimitte omnia peccata mea.

[text also given in the motet in German]

Leiden und Bedrängnis meiner Seele, sie vermehrten sich: aus der
Not und Drangsal des Lebens rette mich, du Gott und Herr. Sieh', wie mein
Herz Verzagen füllet, sieh' die schweren Kämpfe, und vergieb mir jede
Schuld, jegliche Torheit.

An die Musik

Franz von Schober (1796-1882)
Franz Schubert, D. 547, Op. 88, no. 4, 1817
[solo song version]

Du holde Kunst, in wieviel grauen Stunden,
Wo mich des Lebens wilder Kreis umstrickt,
Hast du mein Herz zu warmer Lieb' entzunden,
Hast mich in eine bess're Welt entrückt!

Oft hat ein Seufzer, deiner Harf' entfloßen,
Ein süßer, heiliger Akkord von dir,
Den Himmel bess'rer Zeiten mir erschloßen,
Du holde Kunst, ich danke dir dafür!

Litanei auf das Fest Allerseelen

Johann Georg Jacobi (1740-1814)
Franz Schubert, D. 343, 1816 [solo song]

Ruh'n in Frieden alle Seelen,
Die vollbracht ein banges Quälen,
Die vollendet süßen Traum,
Lebenssatt, geboren kaum,
Aus der Welt hinüber schieden:
Alle Seelen ruh'n in Frieden!

Liebevoller Mädchen Seelen
Deren Tränen nicht zu zählen,
Die ein falscher Freund verließ,
Und die blinde Welt verstieß:
Alle, die von hinnen schieden:
Alle Seelen ruh'n in Frieden!

Und die nie der Sonne lachten,
Unterm Mond auf Dornen wachten,
Gott, im reinen Himmelslicht,
Einst zu sehn vom Angesicht:
Alle, die von hinnen schieden:
Alle Seelen ruh'n in Frieden!

Zum Sanctus

(from *Deutsche Messe*, D. 872)
Johann Philipp Neumann (1774-1849)
Franz Schubert, 1827

Heilig, heilig, heilig,
heilig ist der Herr!
Heilig, heilig, heilig,
heilig ist nur Er!
Er, der nie begonnen,
Er, der immer war,
Ewig ist und waltet,
sein wird immerdar.

Heilig, heilig, heilig,
heilig ist der Herr!
Heilig, heilig, heilig,
heilig ist nur Er!
Allmacht, Wunder, Liebe,
alles rings umher!
Heilig, heilig, heilig,
heilig ist der Herr!

An Webers Grabe

Text: Richard Wagner
Richard Wagner, 1844

Hebt an den Sang, ihr Zeugen dieser Stunde,
die uns so ernst, so feierlich erregt!
Dem Wort, den Tönen jetzt vertraut die Kunde des Hochgefühls,
das uns're Brust bewegt!
Nicht trauert mehr die deutsche Mutter Erde
um den geliebten, weit entrückten Sohn;
nicht blickt sie mehr mit sehnender Gebärde hin übers Meer,
zum fernen Albion: aufs Neu' nahm sie ihn auf in ihren Schoß,
den einst sie aussandt' edel, rein und groß.
Hier, wo der Trauer stumme Zähren flossen,
wo Liebe noch das Teuerste beweint,
hier ward von uns ein edler Bund geschlossen,
der uns um ihn, den Herrlichen, vereint;
hier wallet her, des Bundes Treugenossen,
hier grüßet euch als fromme Pilgerschar,
die schönsten Blüten, die dem Bund entsprossen,
bring opfernd dieser edlen Stätte dar!
Denn hier ruh' Er, bewundert und geliebt,
der unsrem Bund der Weihe Segen gibt!

Aufblick

Joseph von Eichendorff (1788-1857)
[originally entitled *Mittag*]
Hugo Wolf, *6 geistliche Lieder*, no. 1, 1881

Vergeht mir der Himmel
vor Staube schier,
Herr, im Getümmel
zeig' dein Panier!

Wie schwank' ich sündlich,
lässt du von mir:
unüberwindlich,
bin ich mit dir!

Letzte Bitte

Joseph von Eichendorff (1788-1857) from *Der Pilger*
Hugo Wolf, *6 geistliche Lieder*, no. 4, 1881

Wie ein todeswunder Streiter,
der den Weg verloren hat,
schwank' ich nun und kann nicht weiter,
von dem Leben sterbensmatt.
Nacht schon decket alle Müden,
und so still ist's um mich her,
Herr, auch mir gib endlich Frieden,
denn ich wünsch' und hoff' nichts mehr.

Ergebung

Joseph von Eichendorff (1788-1857) from *Der Pilger*
Hugo Wolf, *6 geistliche Lieder*, no. 5, 1881

Dein Wille, Herr, geschehe!
Verdunkelt schweigt das Land.
Im Zug der Wetter sehe
ich schauernd deine Hand.
O mit uns Sündern gehe
erbarmend ins Gericht!
Ich beug' im tiefsten Wehe,
zum Staub mein Angesicht.
Dein Wille, Herr, geschehe!